Marching Wolves

Fumi Nagasaka

KAHL

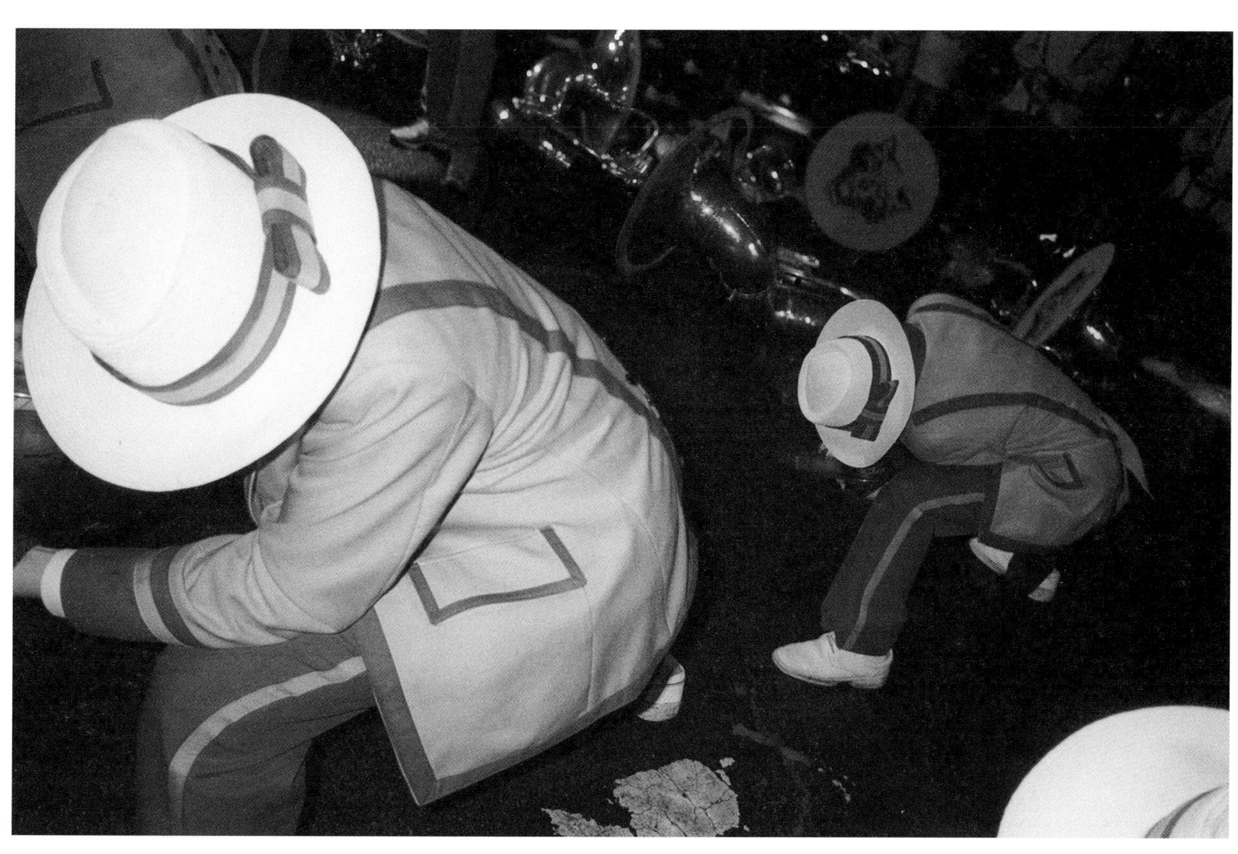

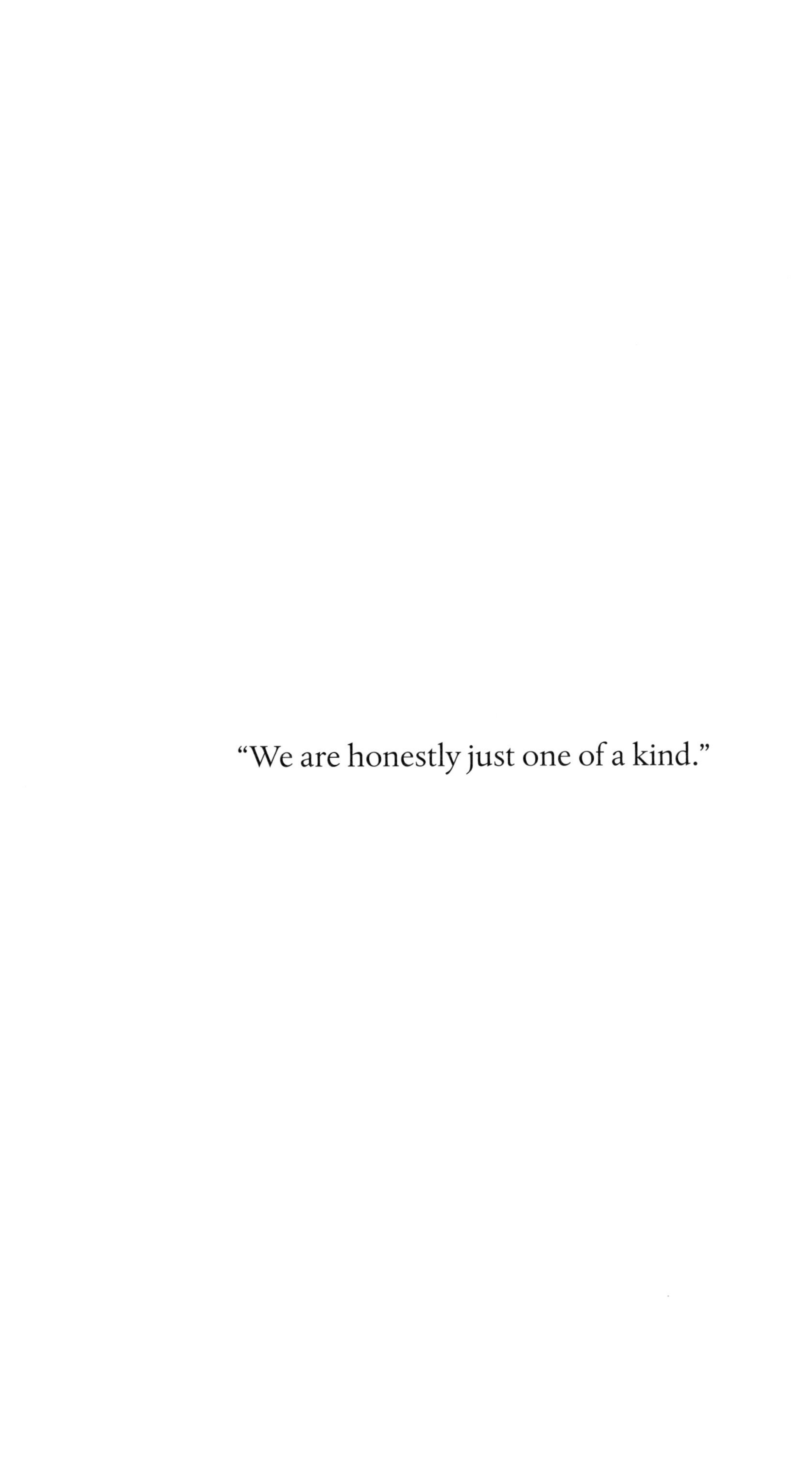

"We are honestly just one of a kind."

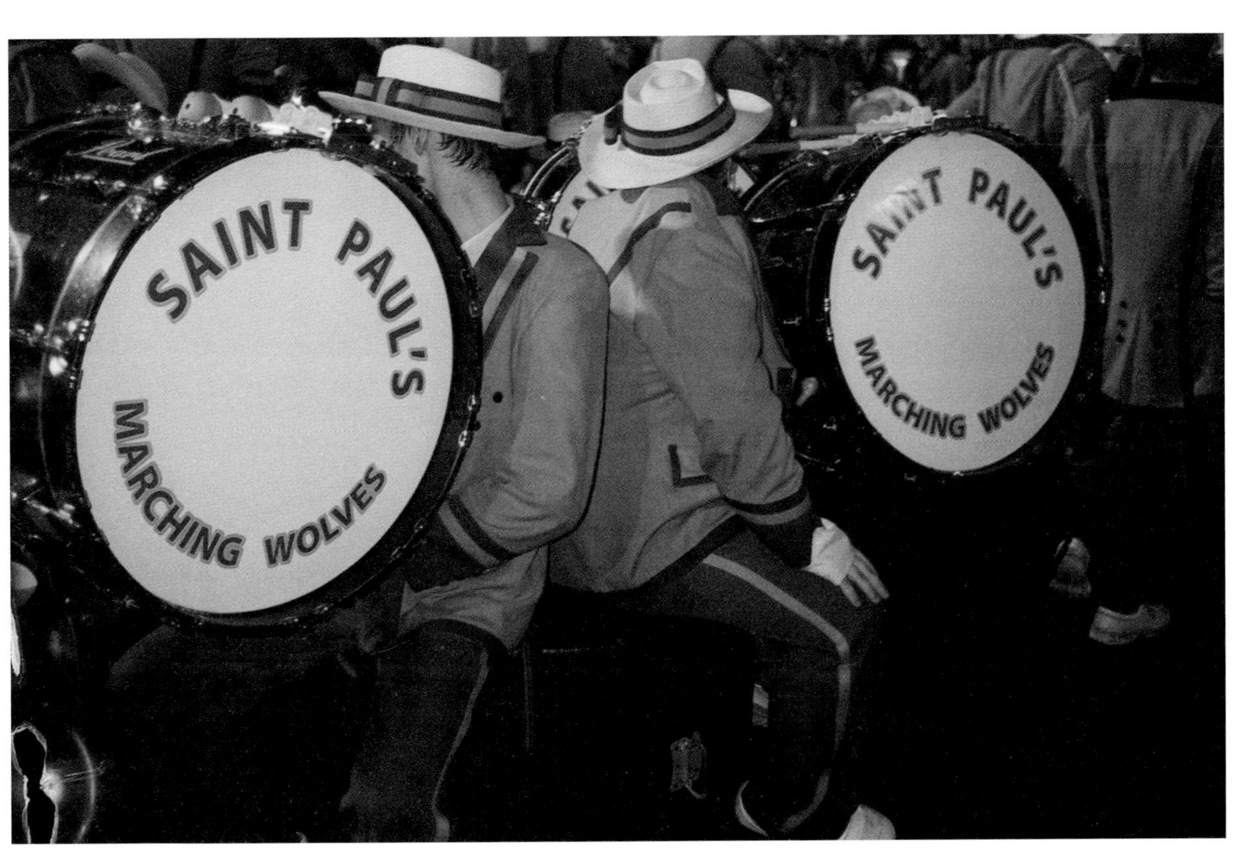
SAINT PAUL'S
MARCHING WOLVES
SAINT PAUL'S
MARCHING WOLVES

Marching bands are the fabric of high school culture, giving students purpose and alumni pride. Saint Paul's is recognized for their signature style.

When bands in New Orleans come marching and dancing down the street, they fill the crowd with the energy and aura of celebration. All the bands provide a spectacle unrivaled in any city in America. The Saint Paul's Marching Wolves, with their iconic uniforms and dances, have been performing at football games and Mardi Gras parades for over 40 years.

In 2017, I travelled to New Orleans to experience the Mardi Gras festival. Saint Paul's Marching Wolves appeared, started to perform in front of me and caught my eye.
I immediately began to search for them, and reached out to Andrew Moran, the Band Director. He agreed for me to come out to visit.

I began to photograph in 2017. In February 2018 and 2020, I returned to shoot during Mardi Gras. Every day, we took a school bus to New Orleans to be on different parade routes over a couple of days.

I was inspired by the energy and tension from the members of the Saint Paul's Marching Wolves and their performance.

Fumi Nagasaka

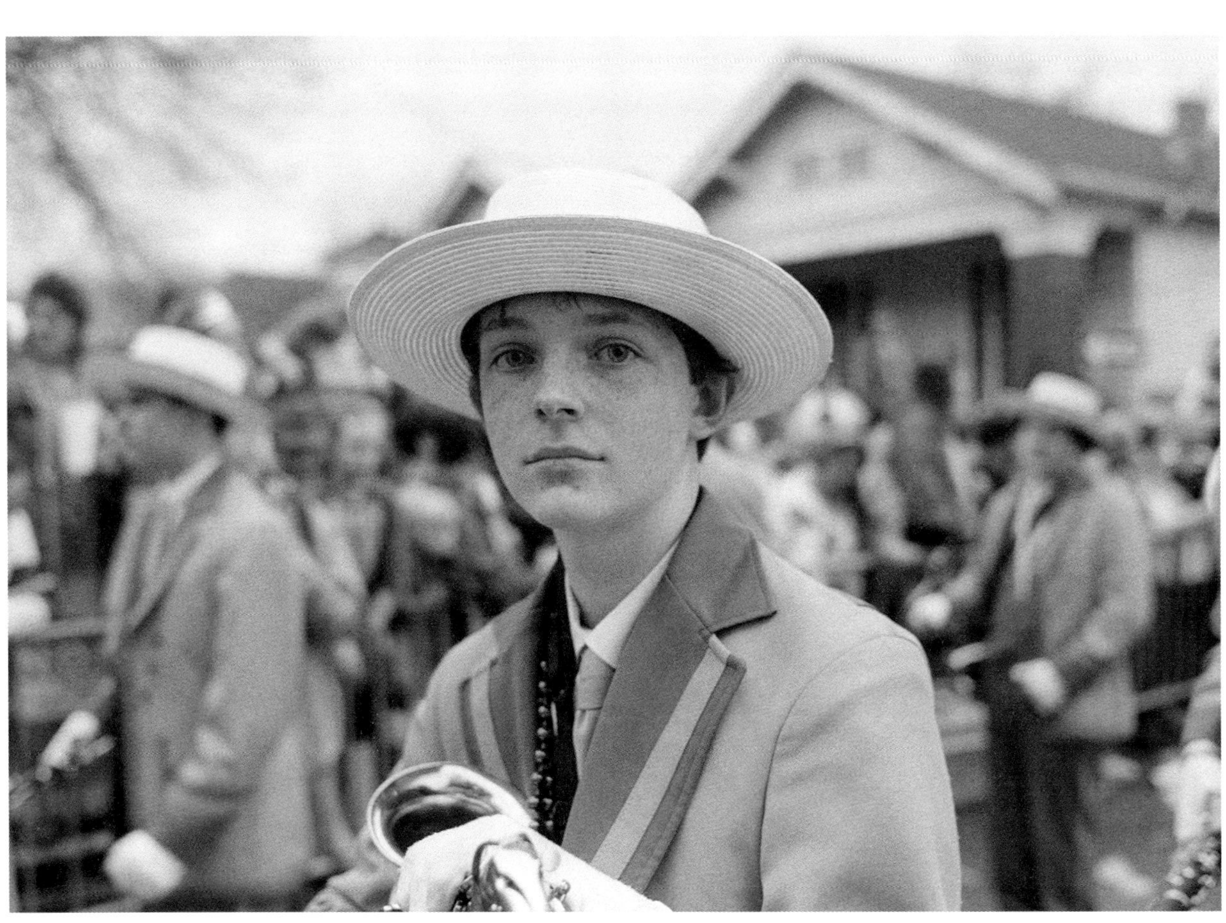

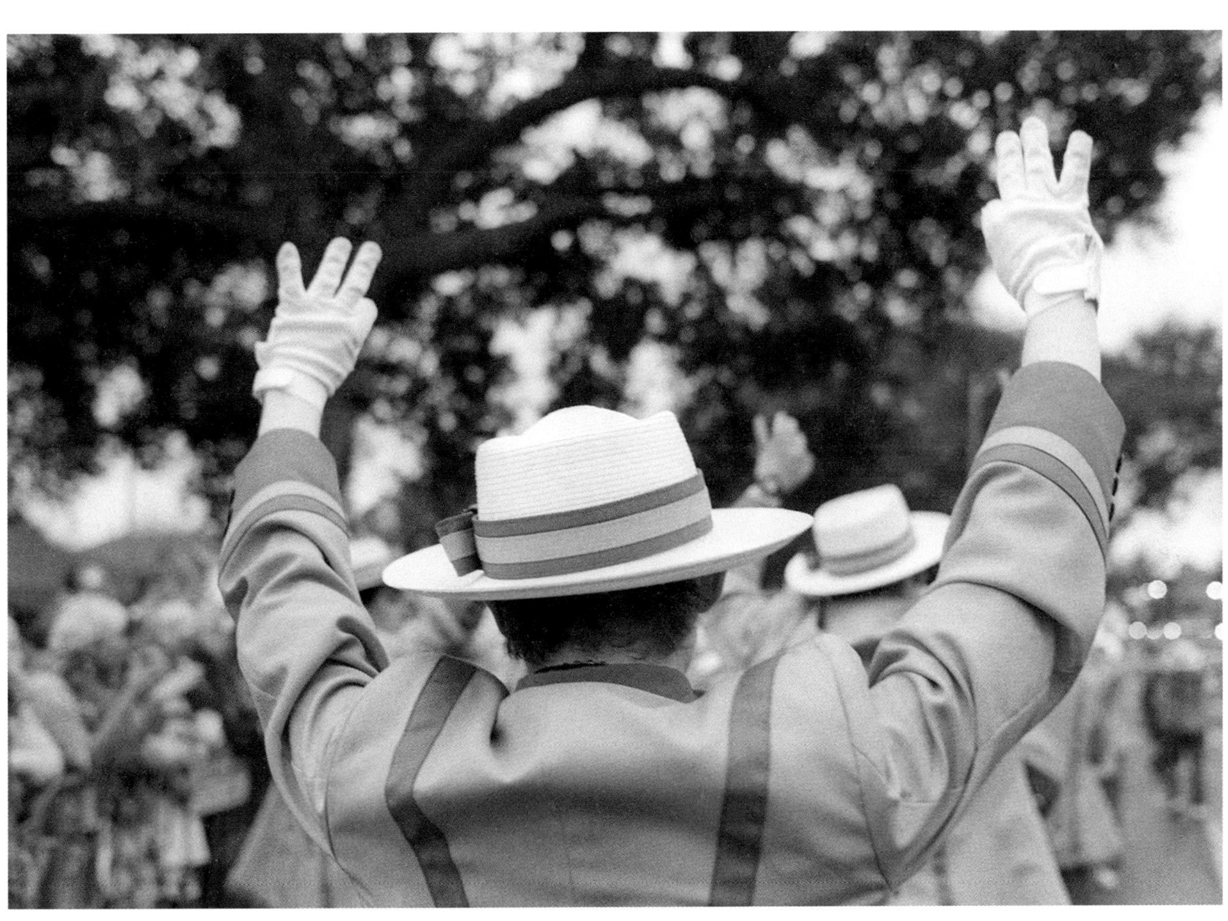

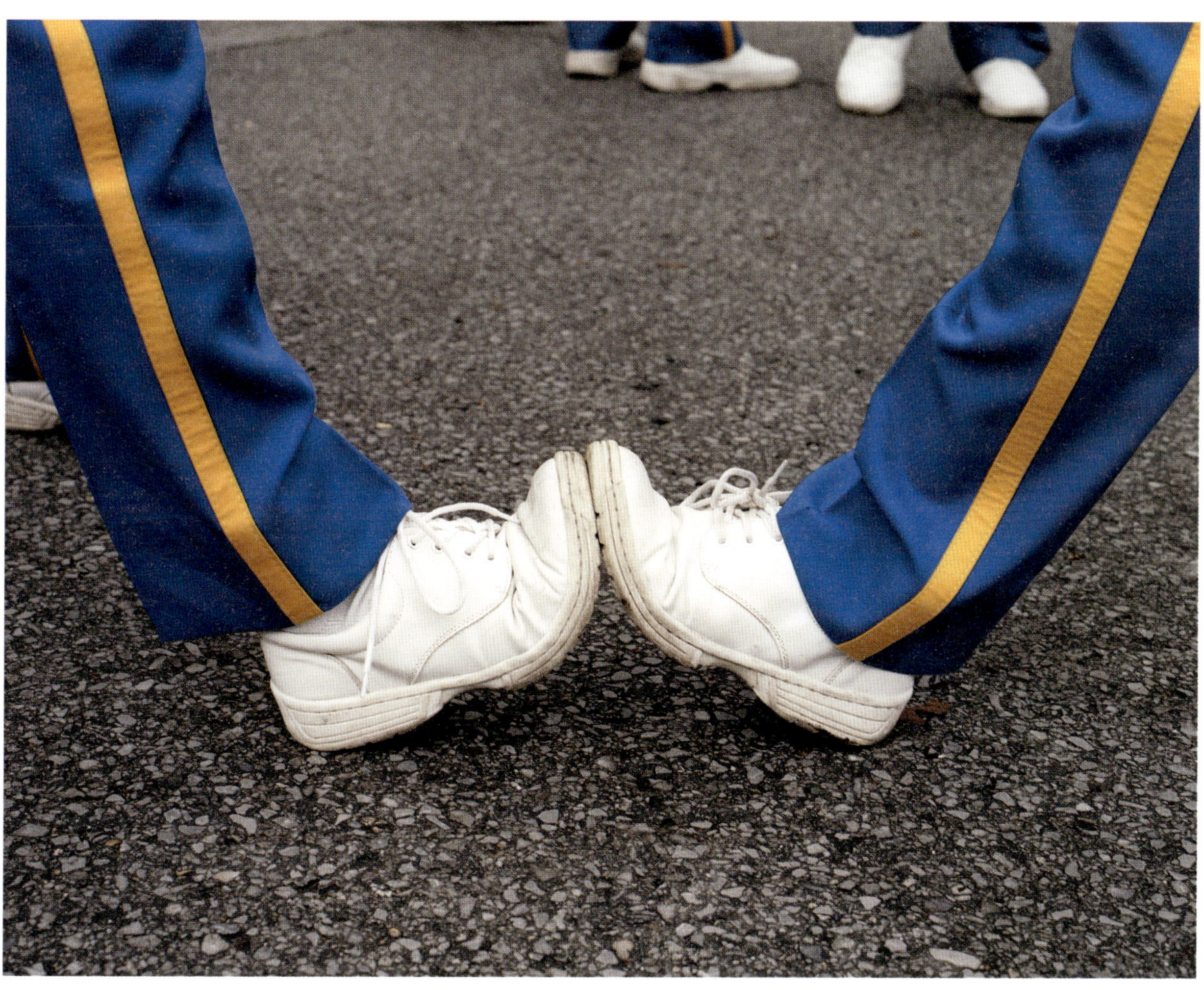

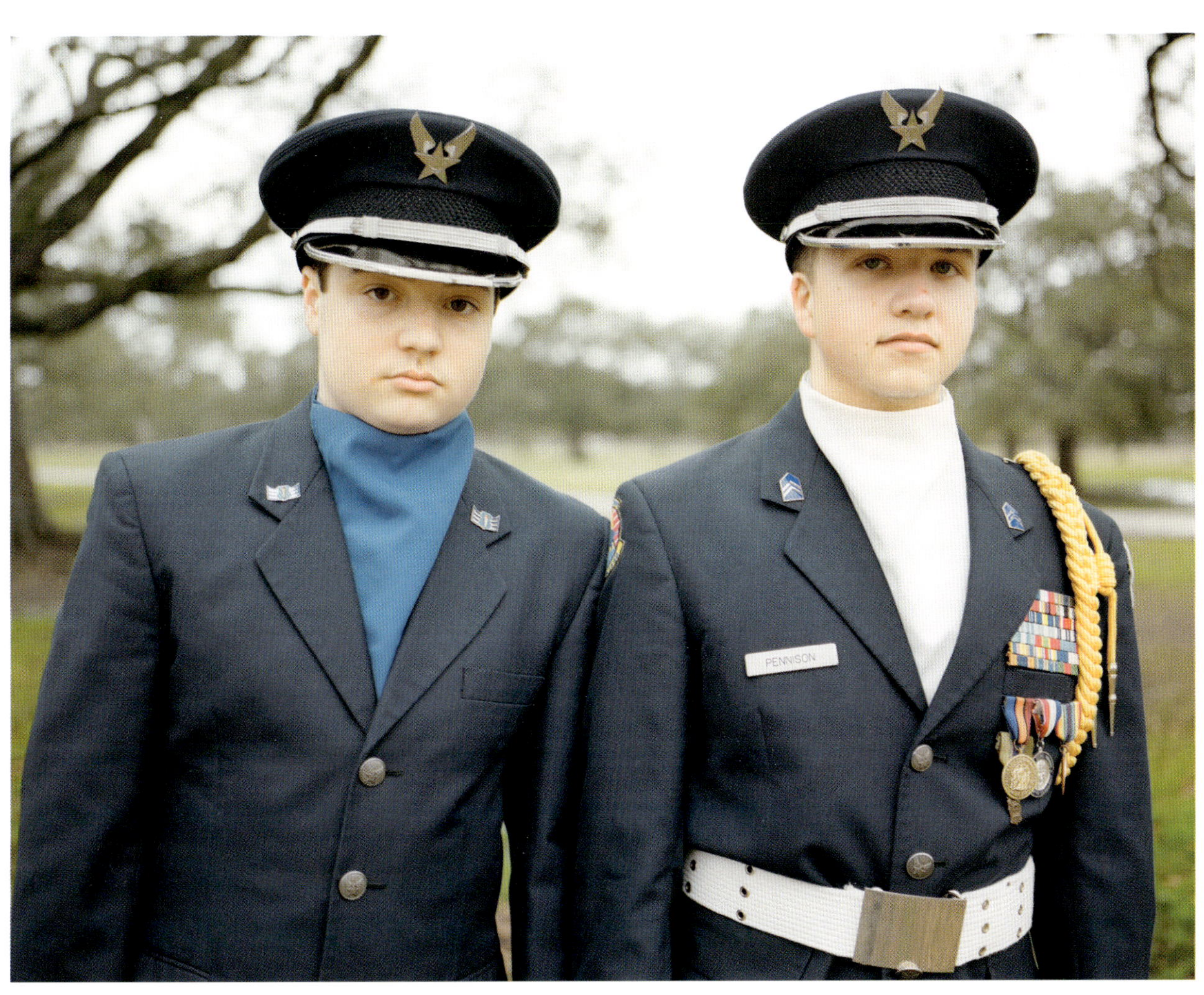
PENNISON

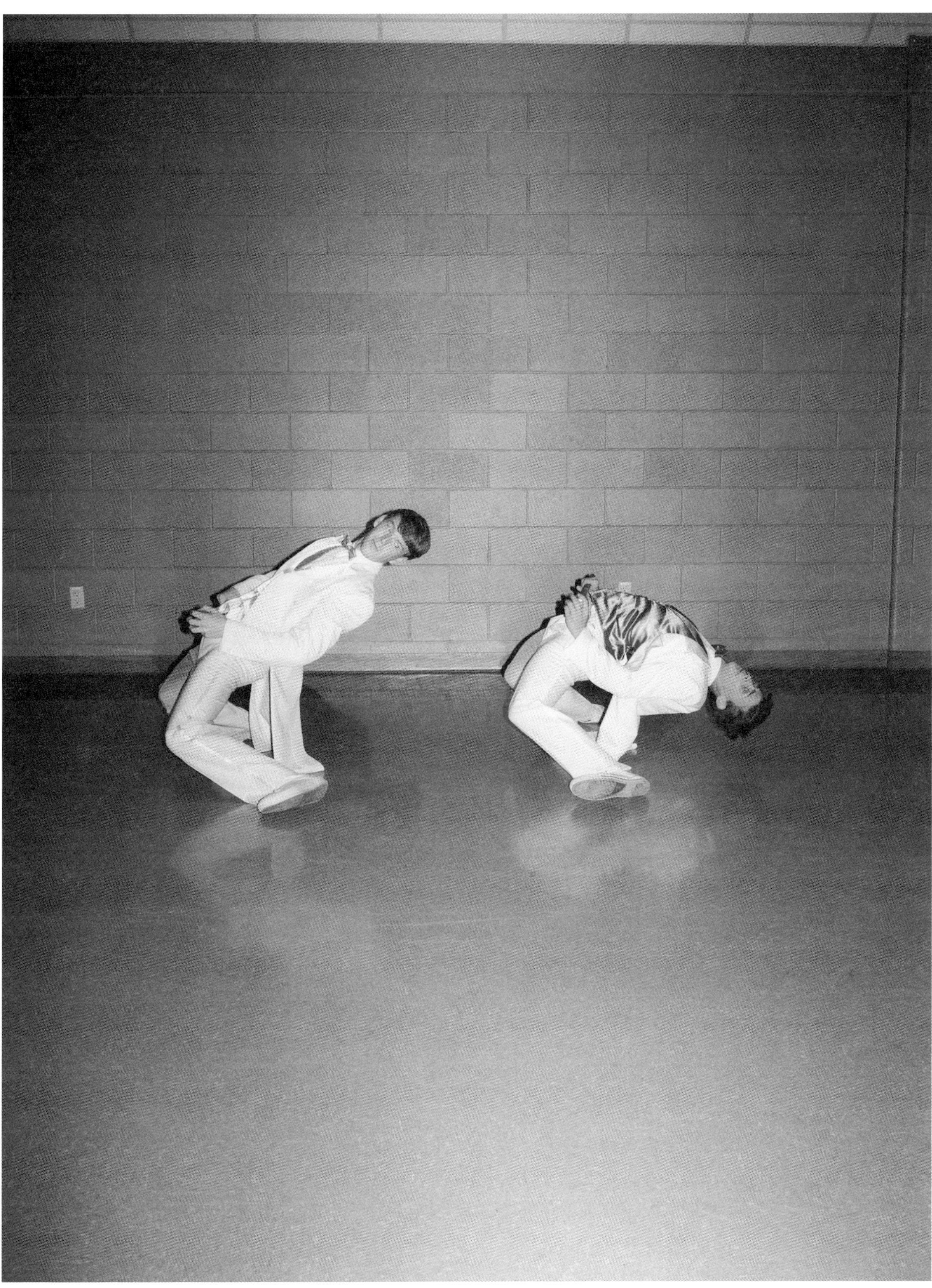

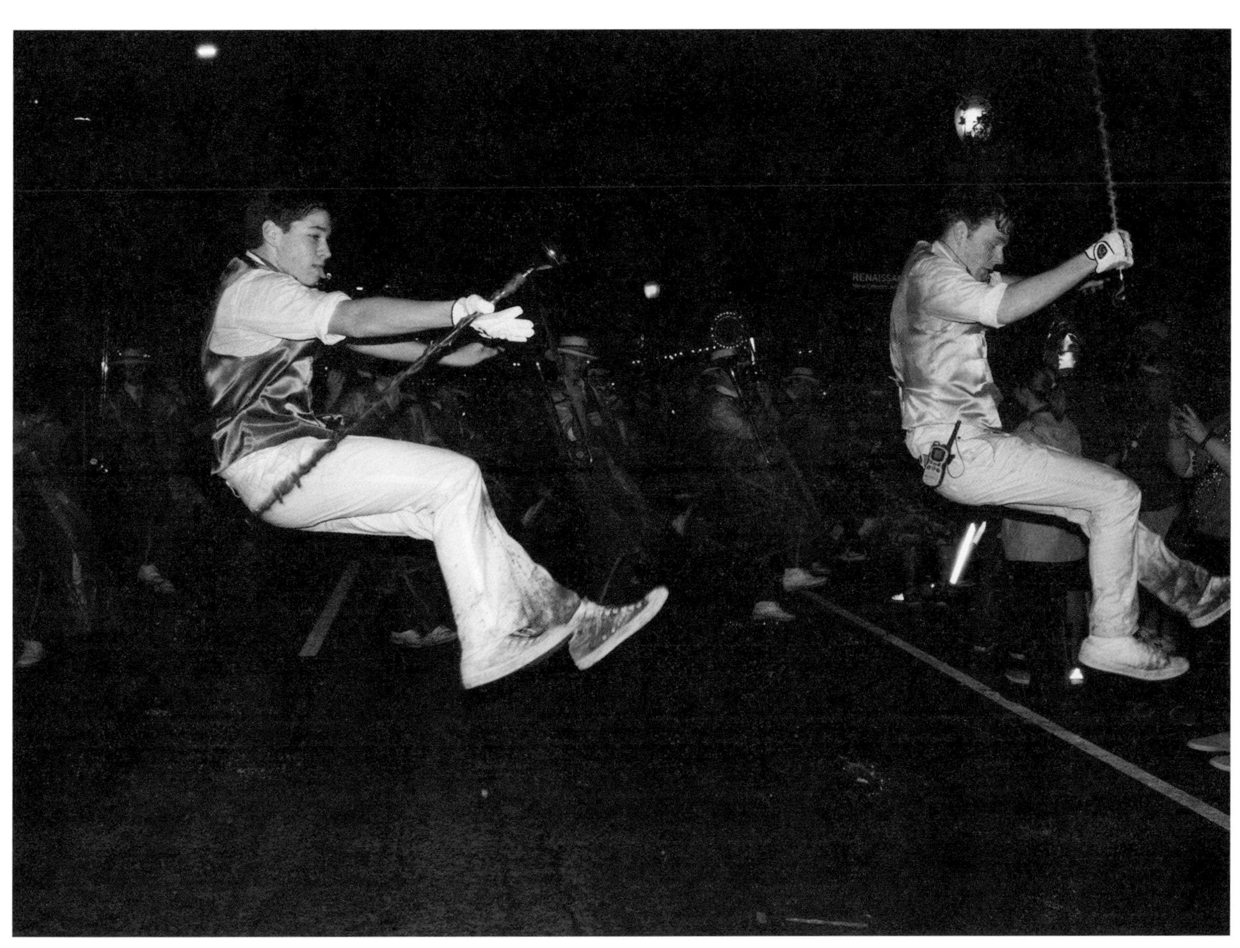

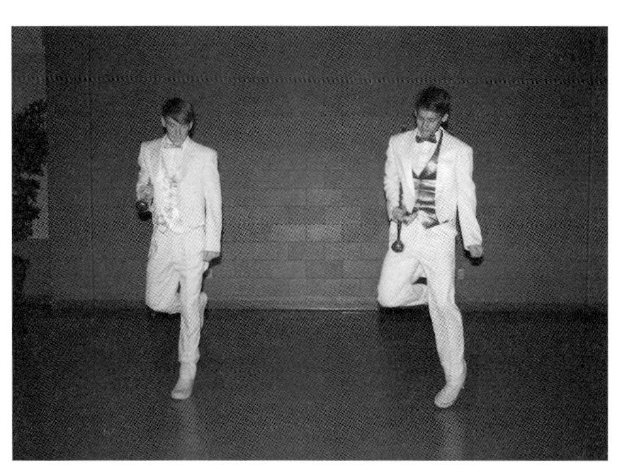
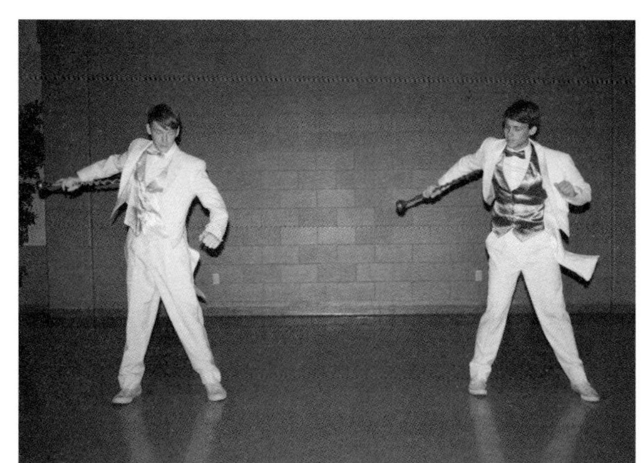
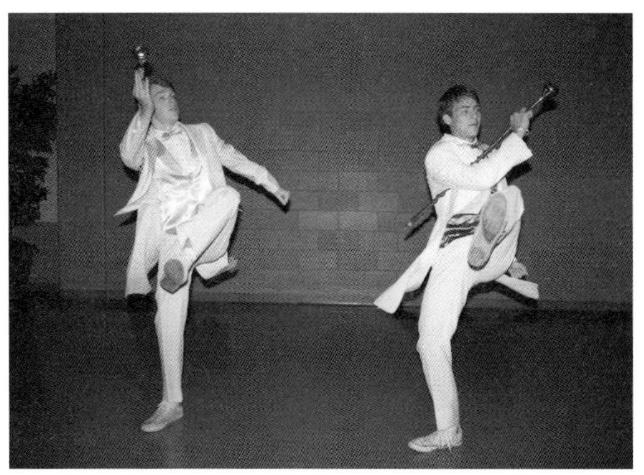
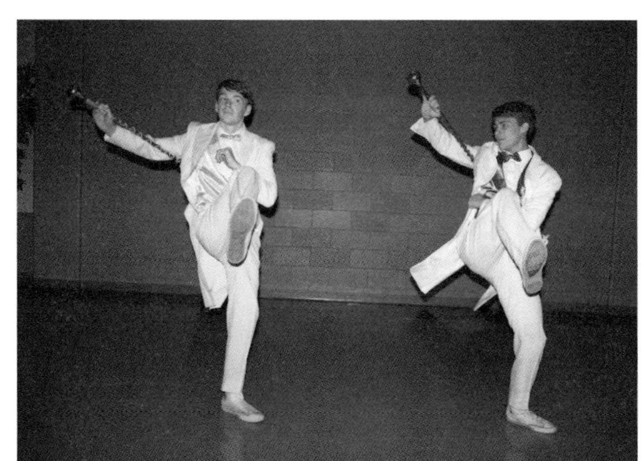

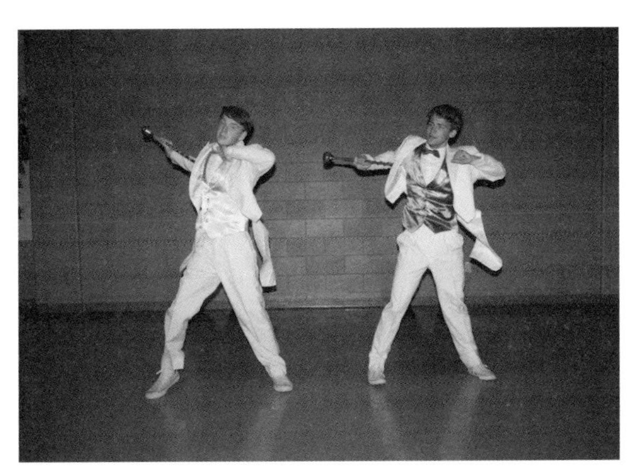
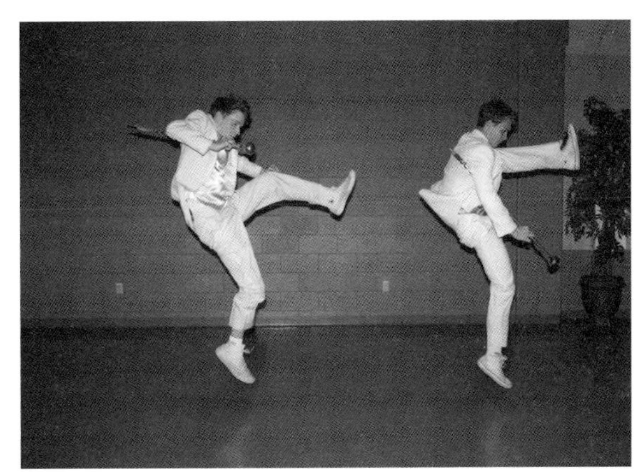
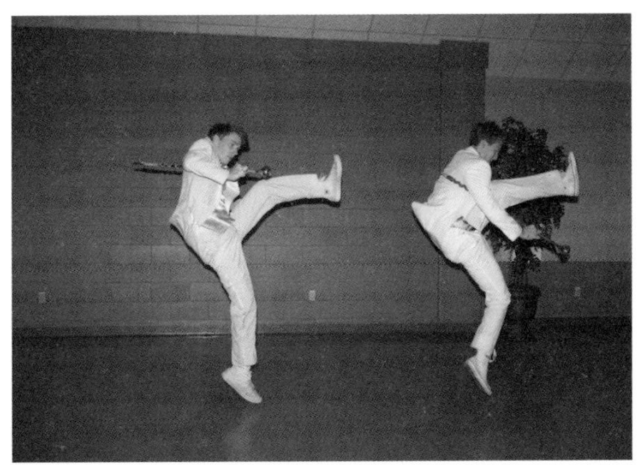
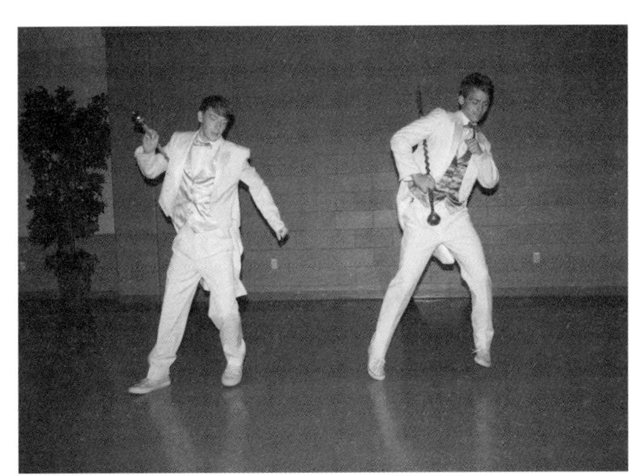

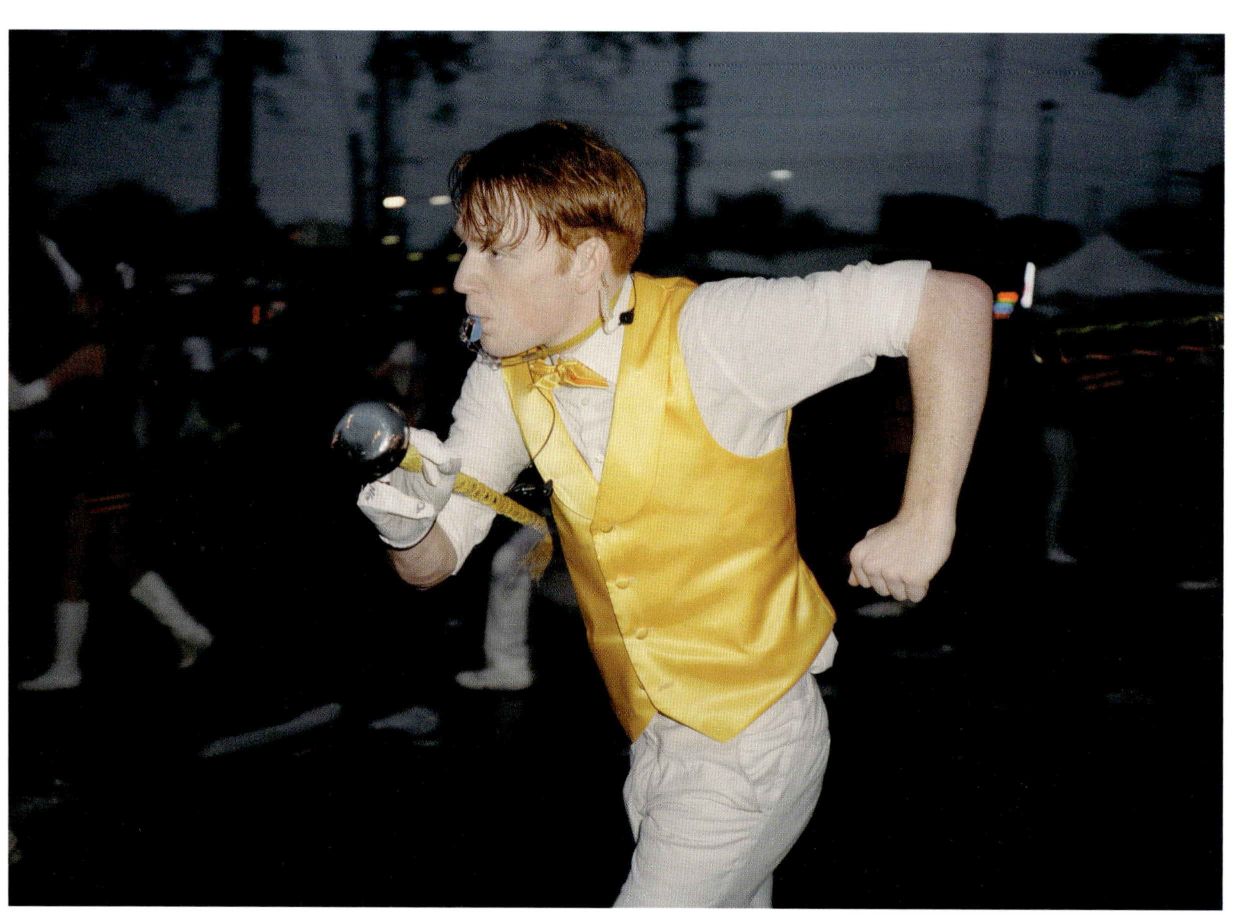

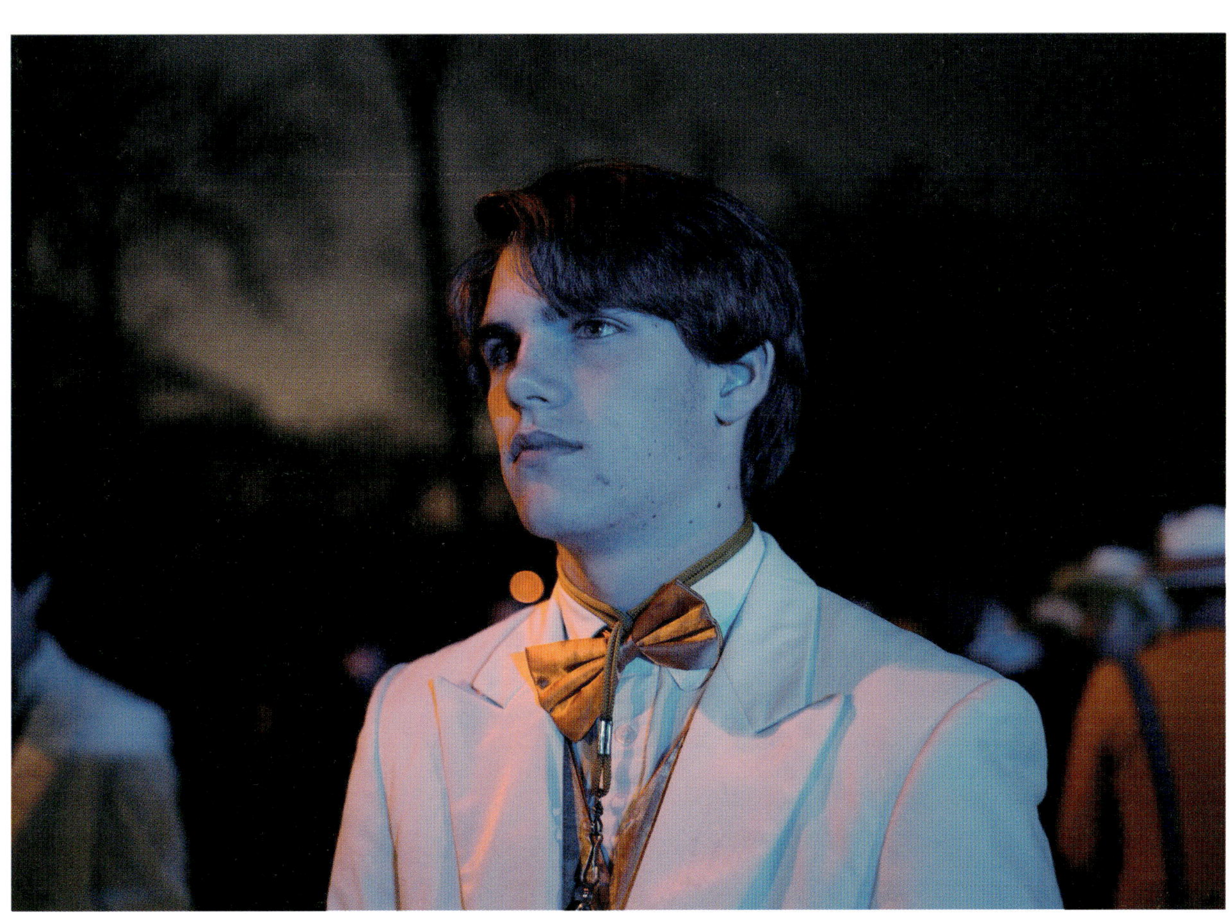

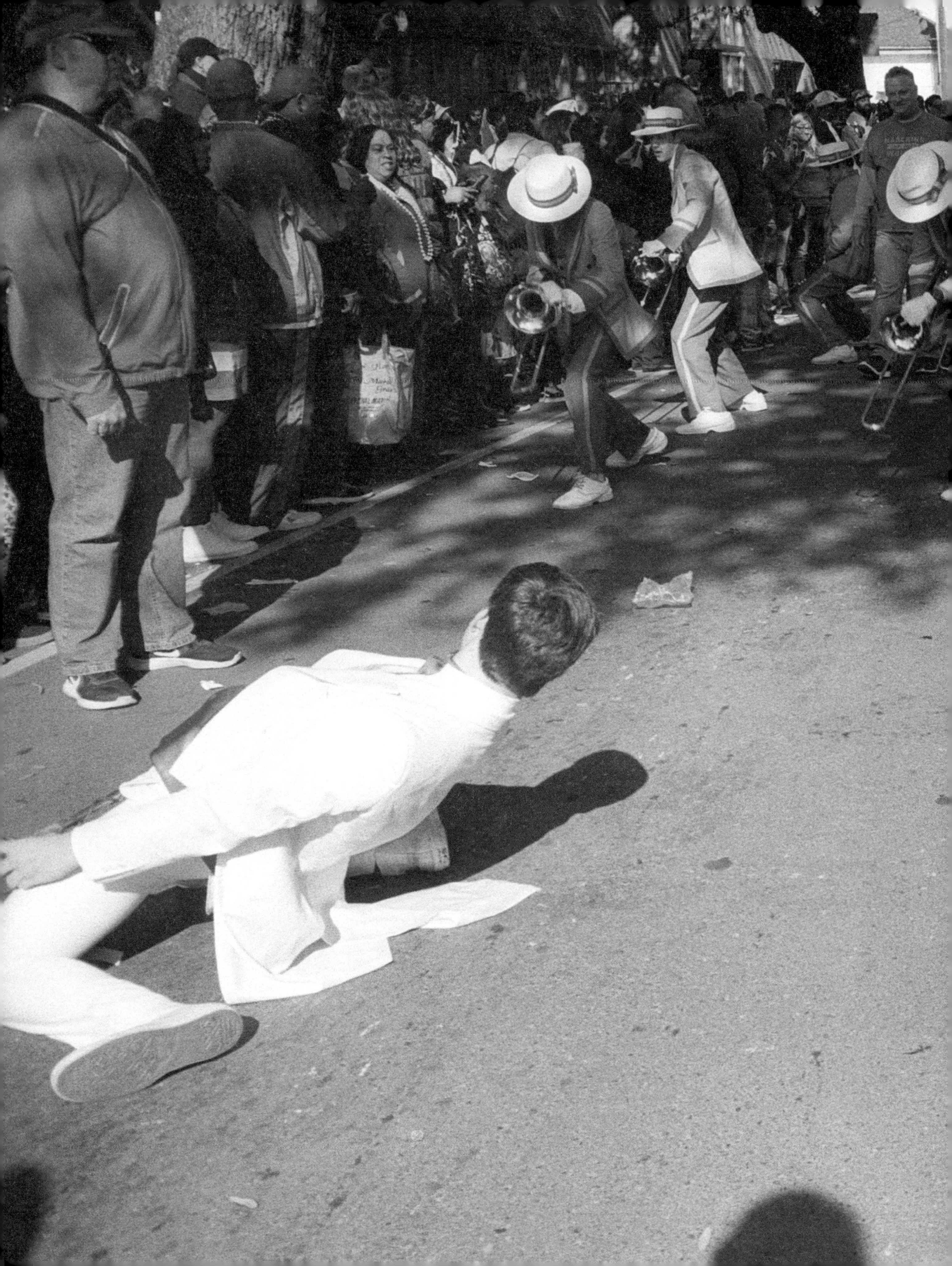

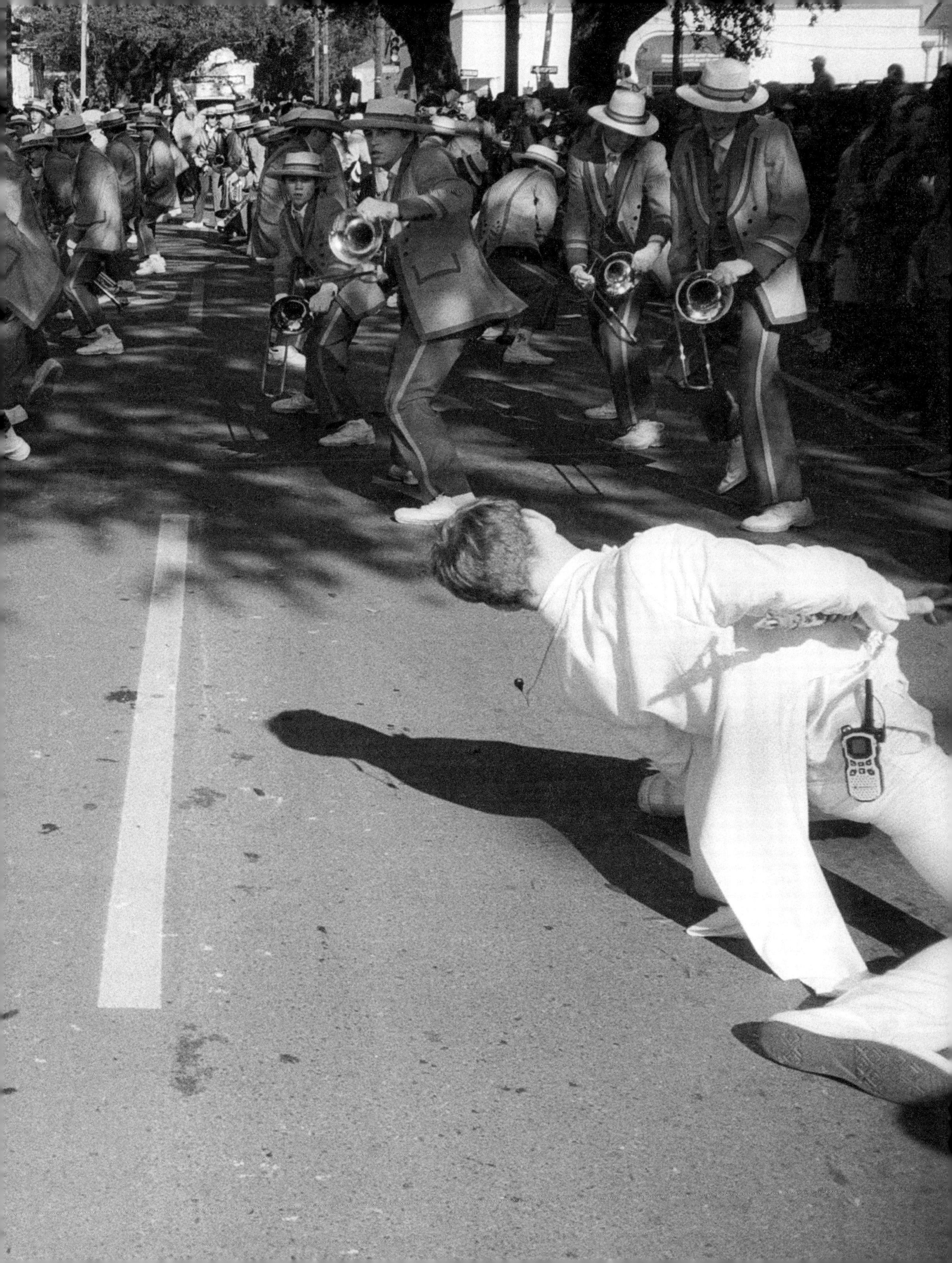

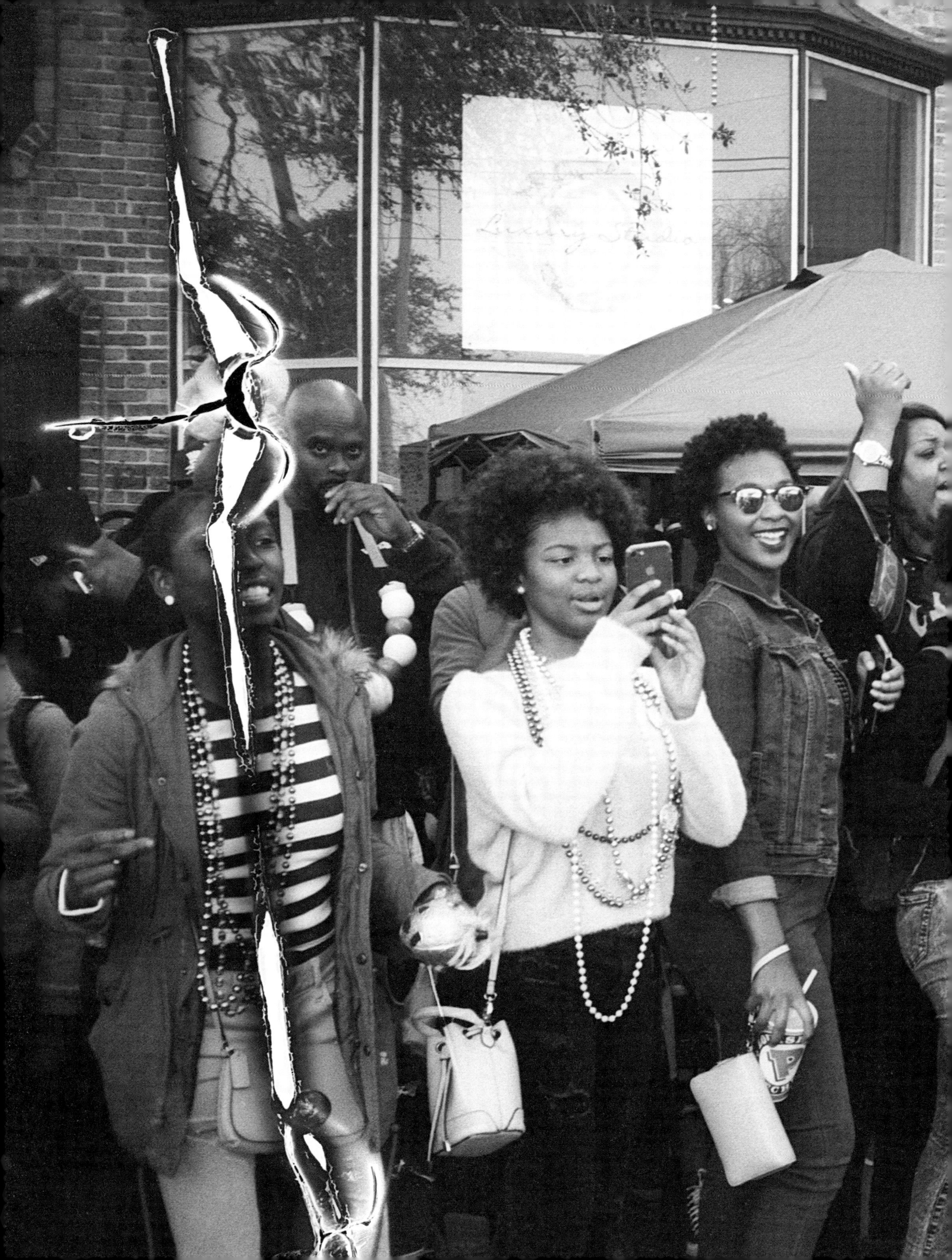

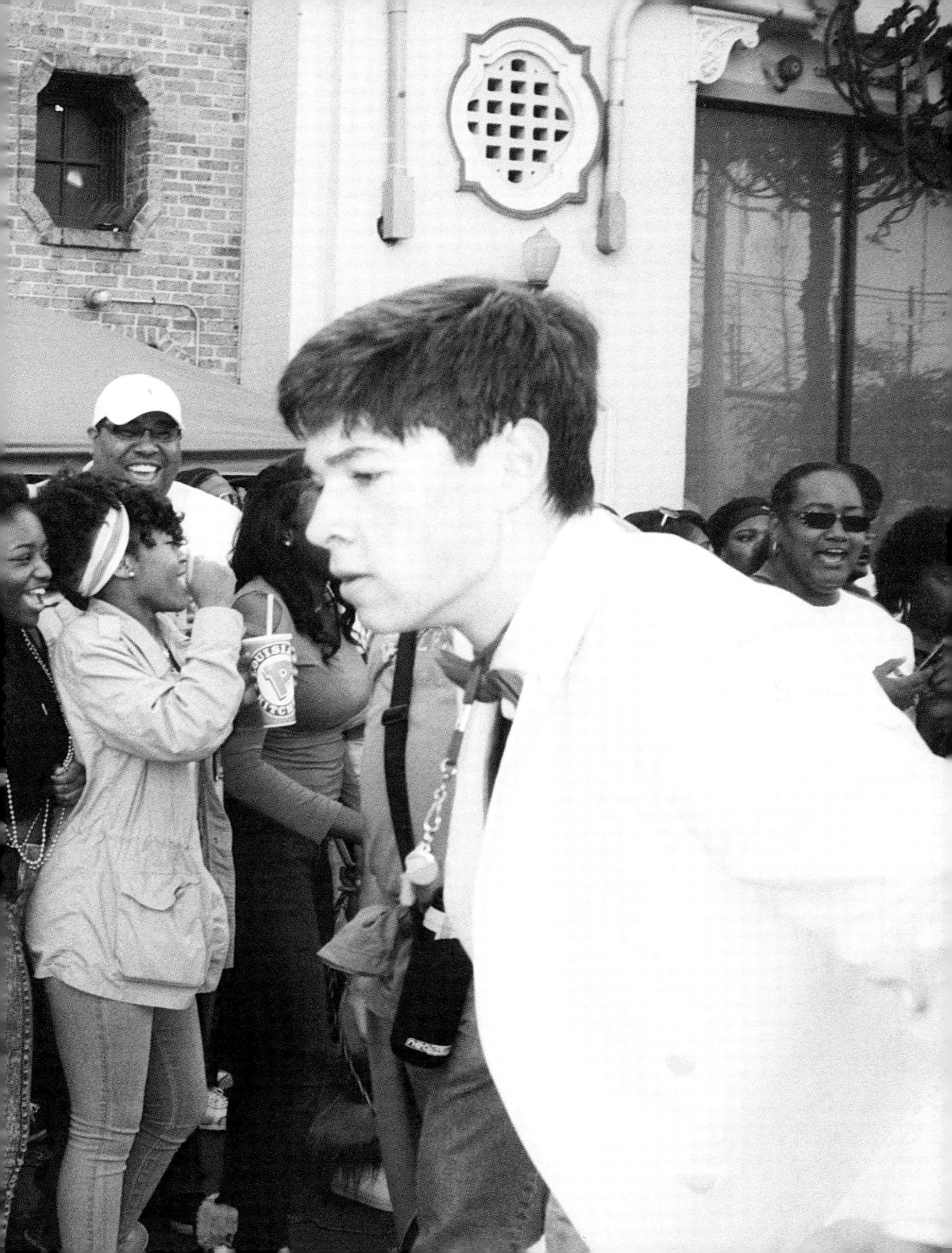

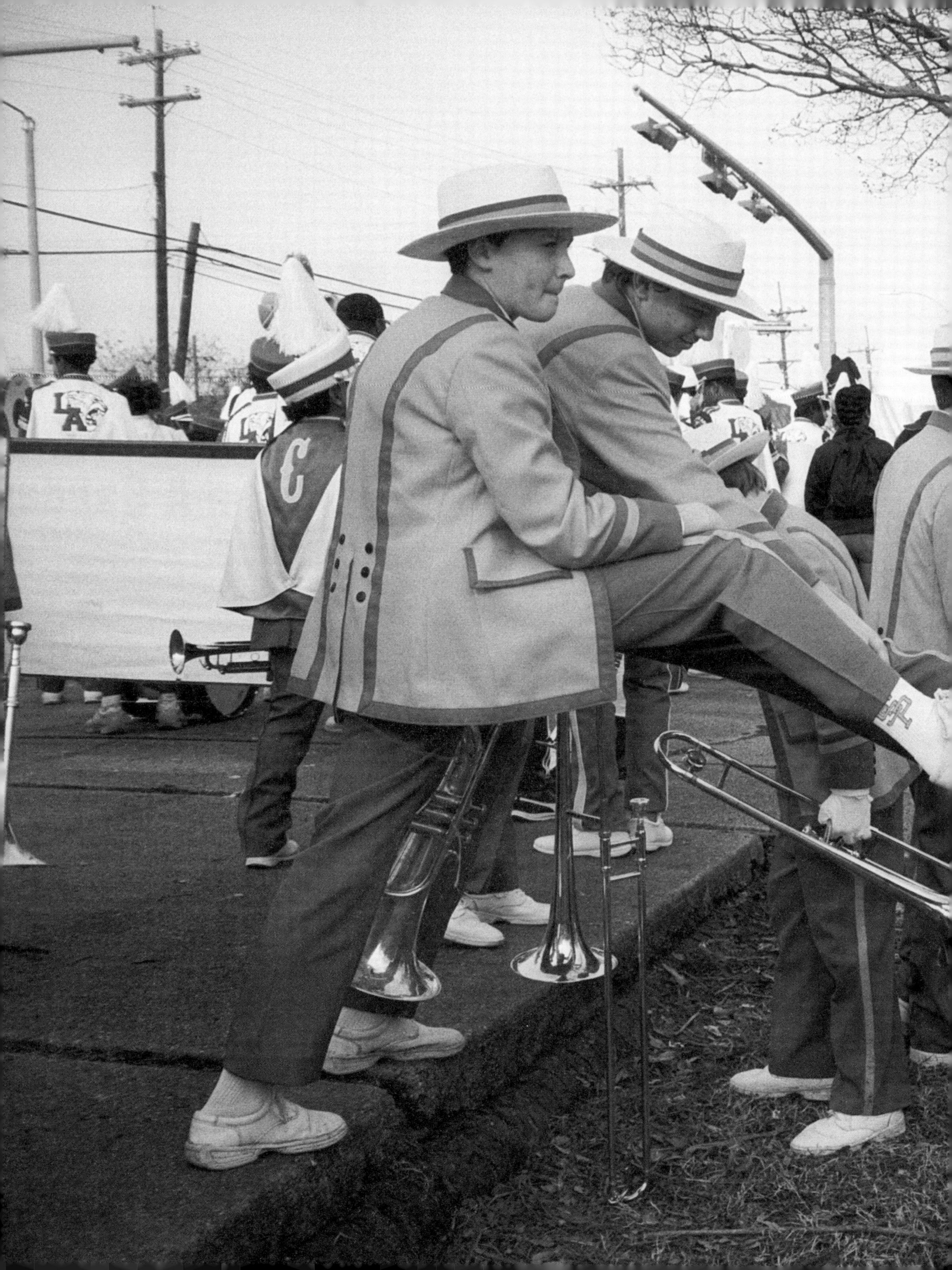

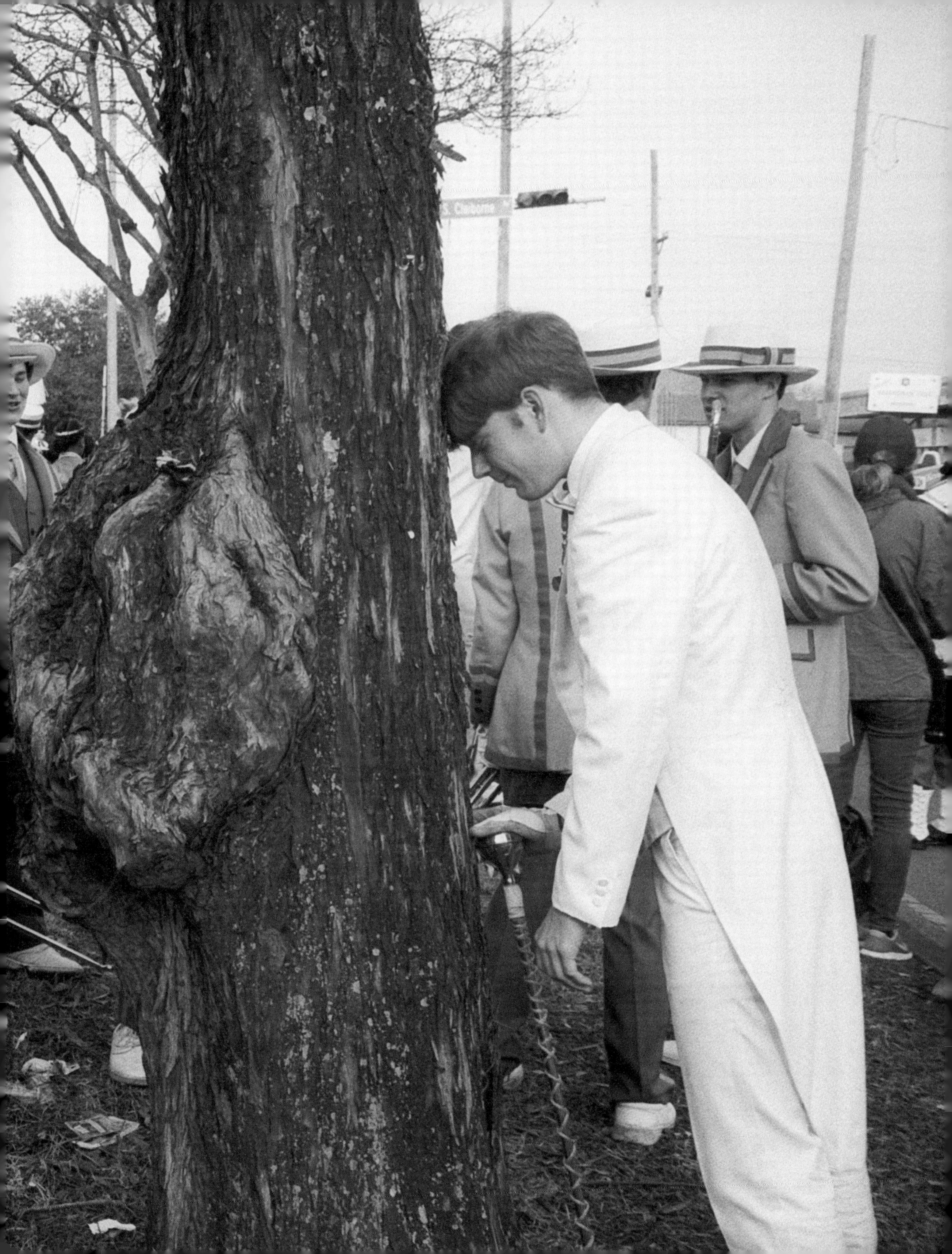

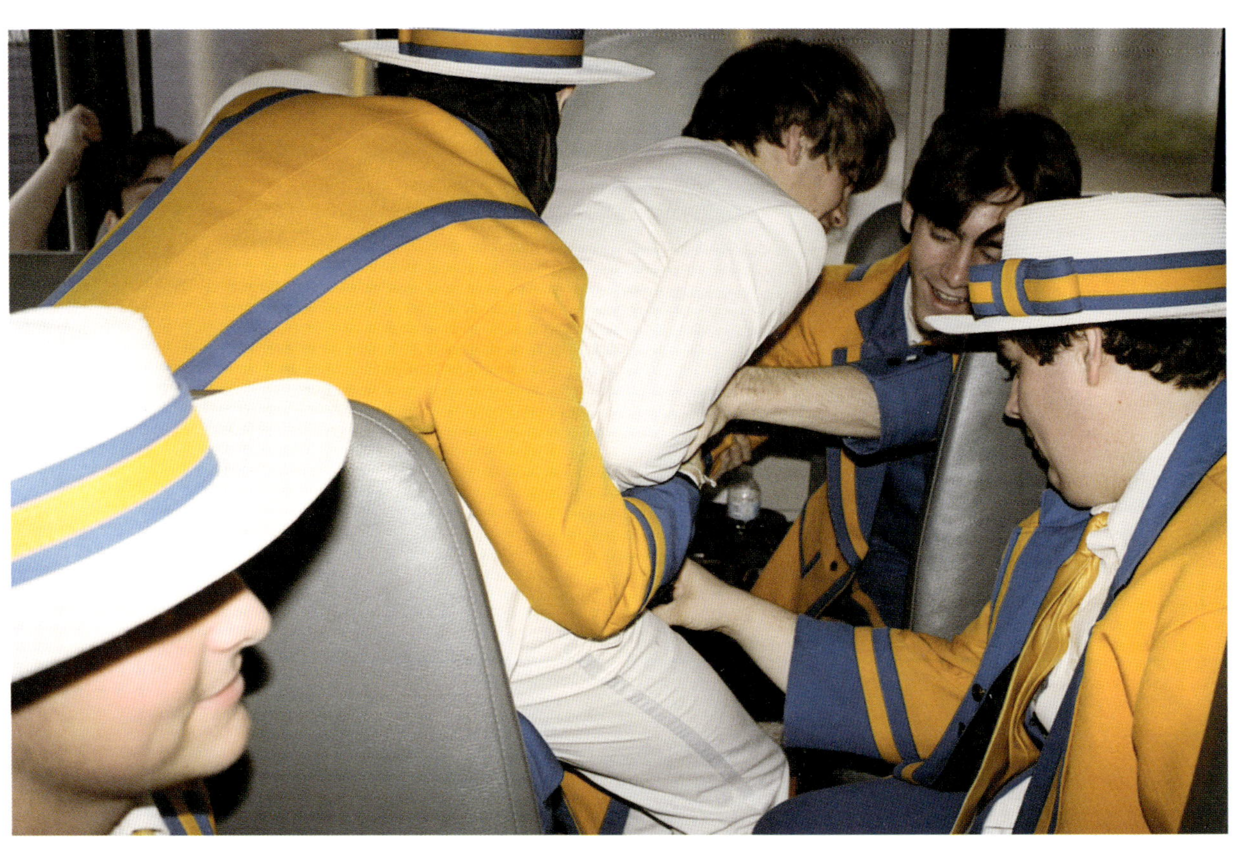

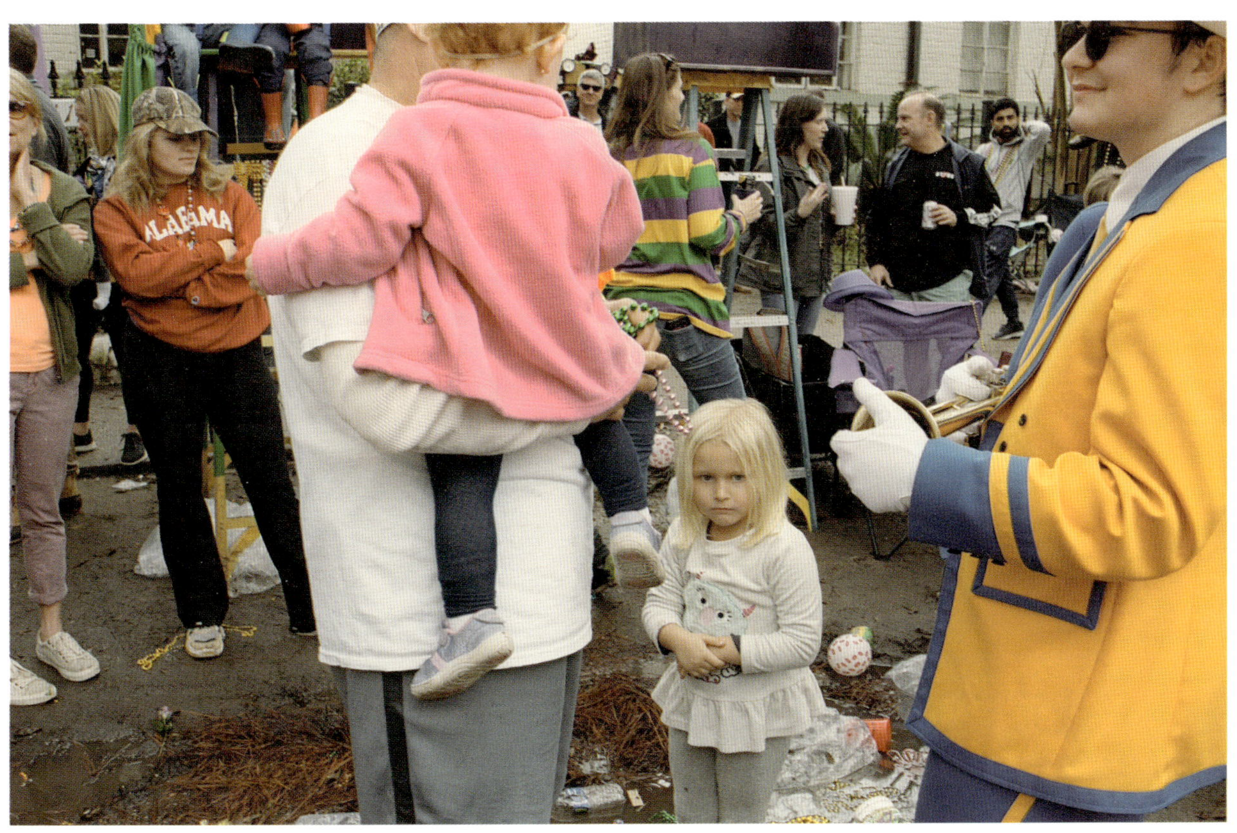

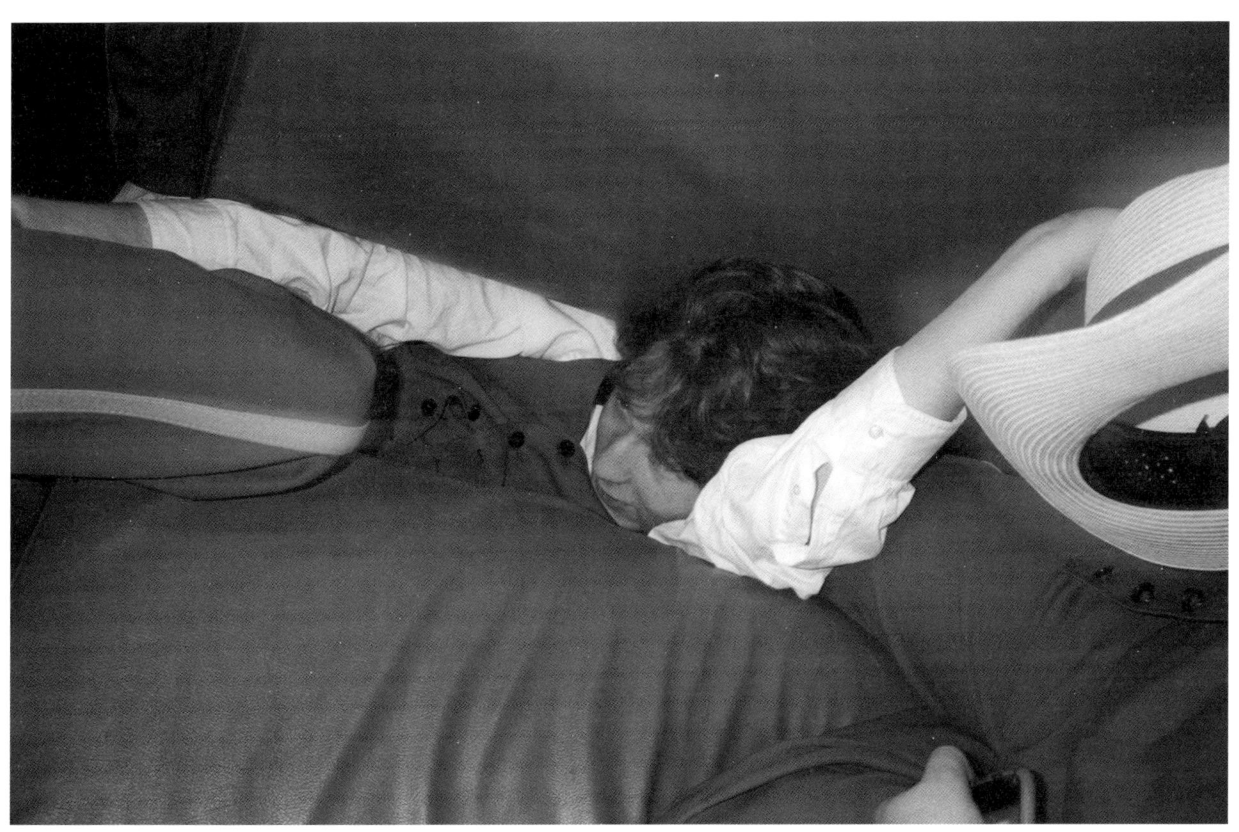

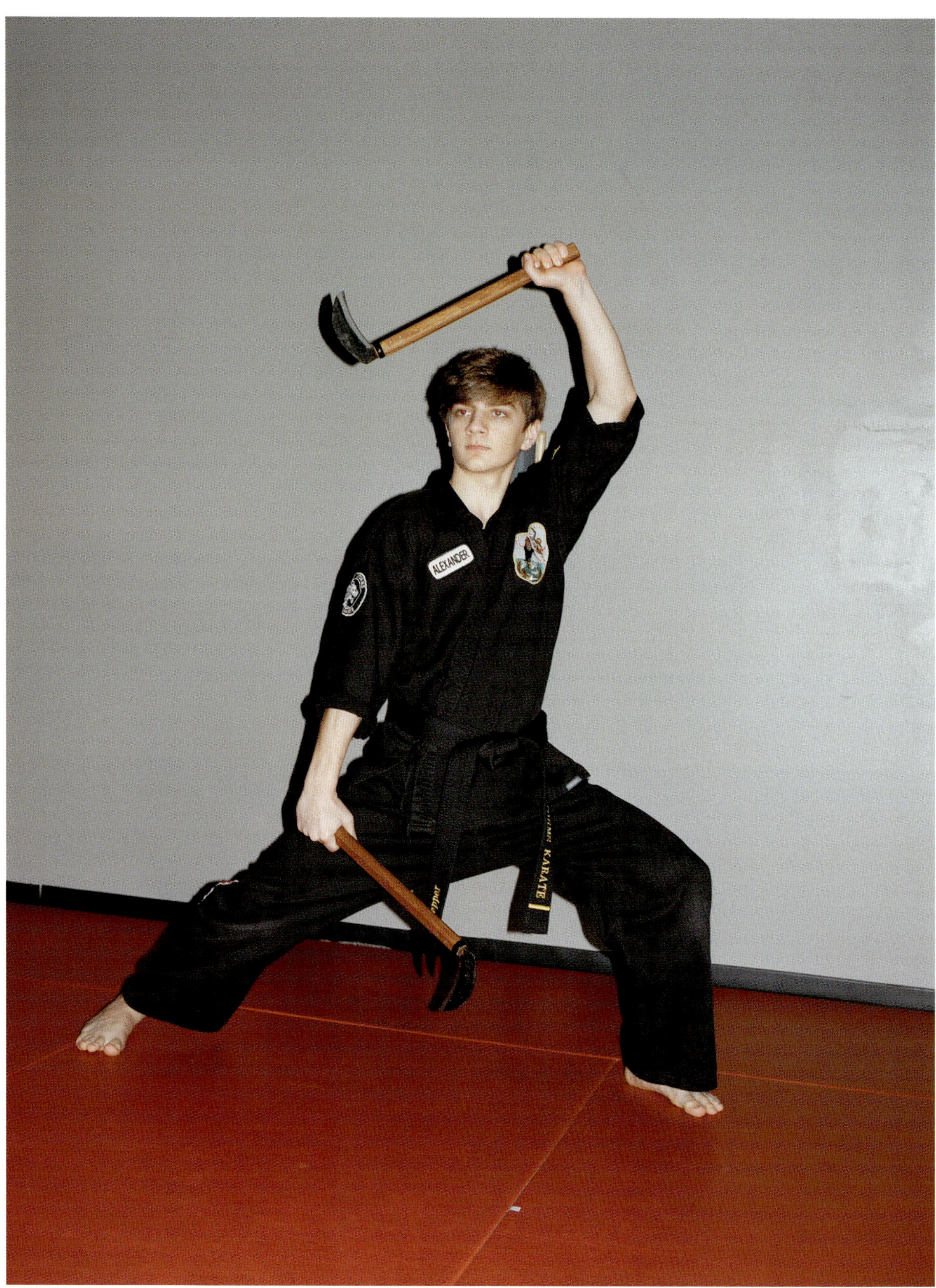

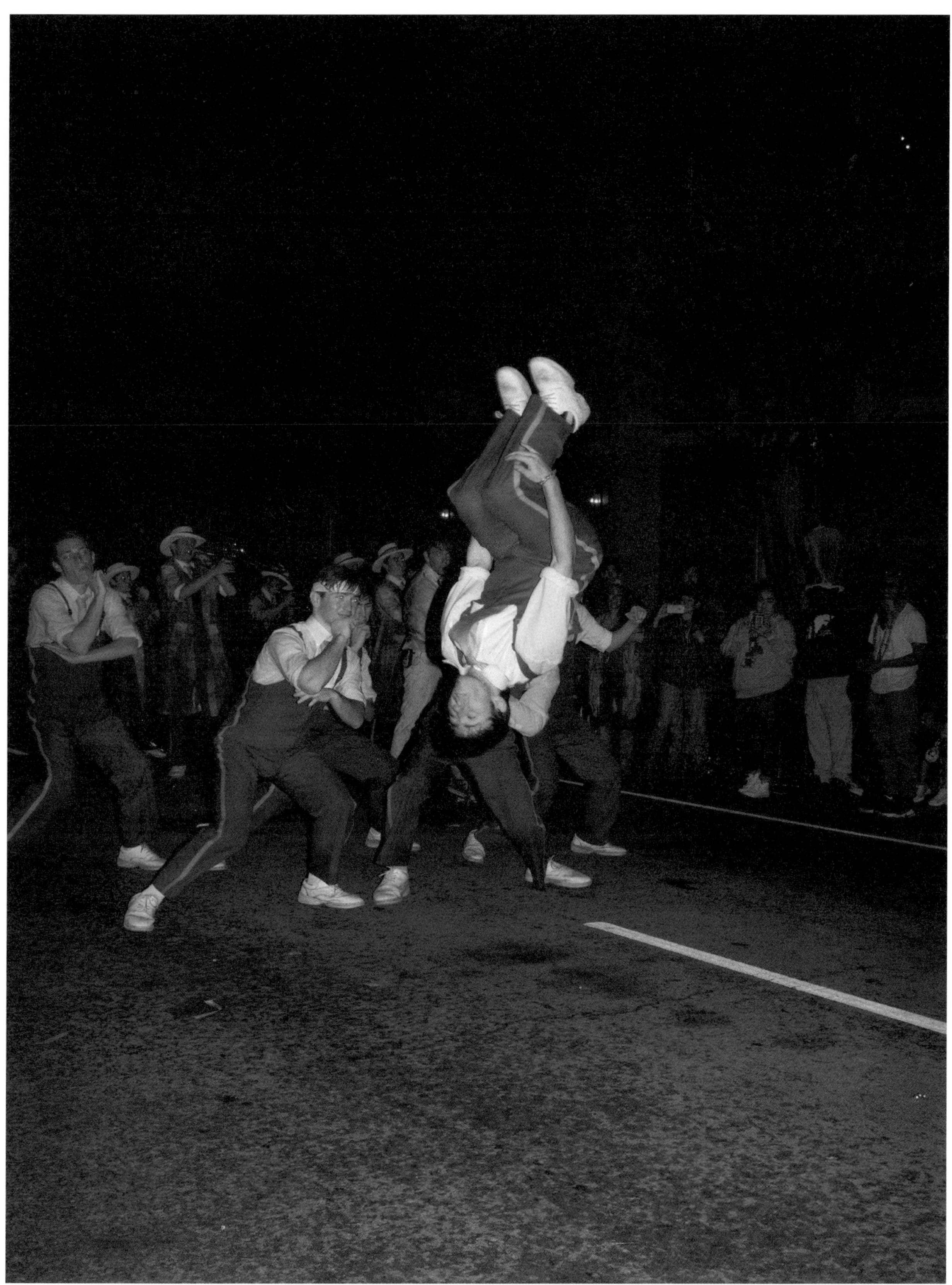

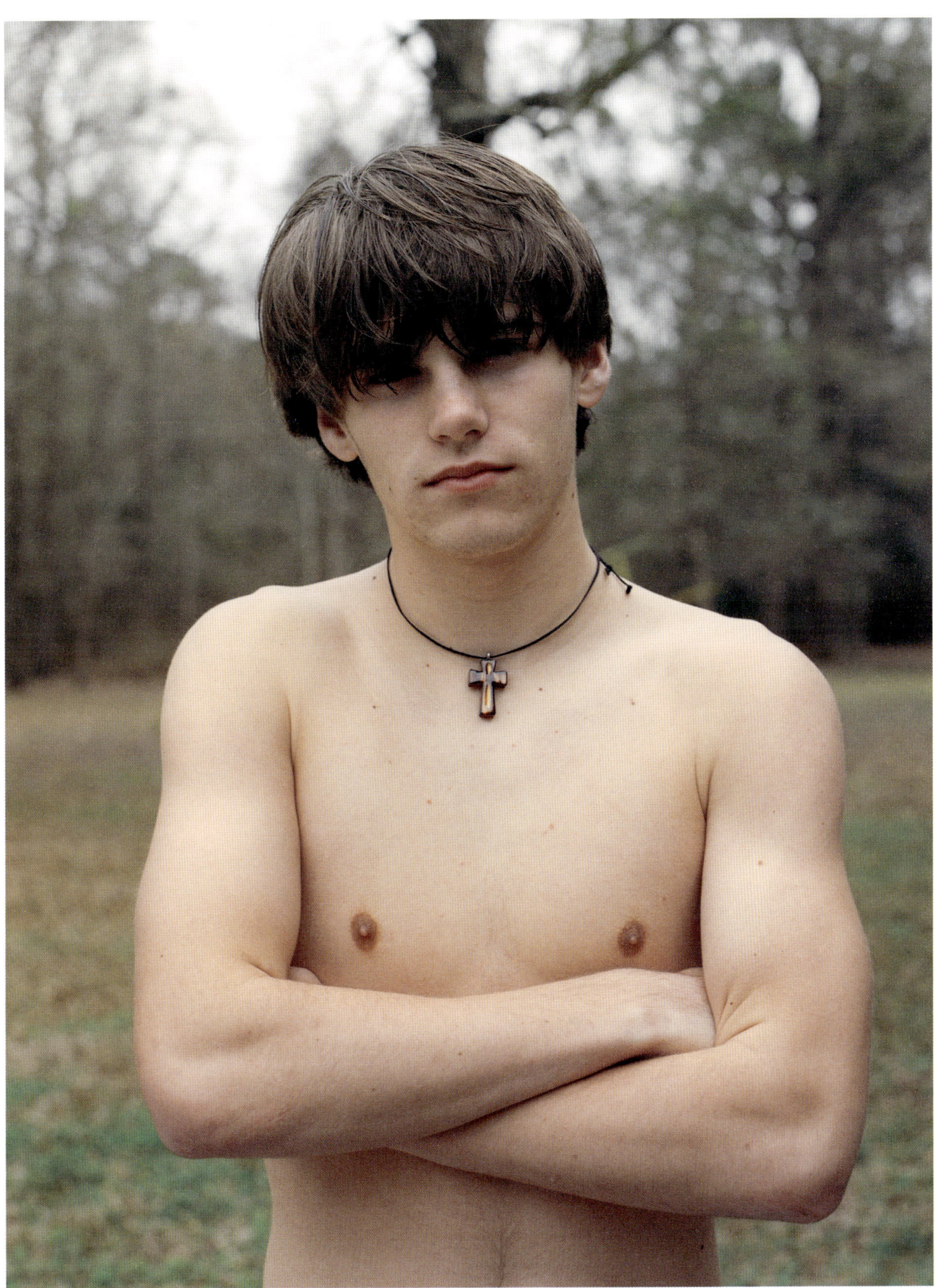

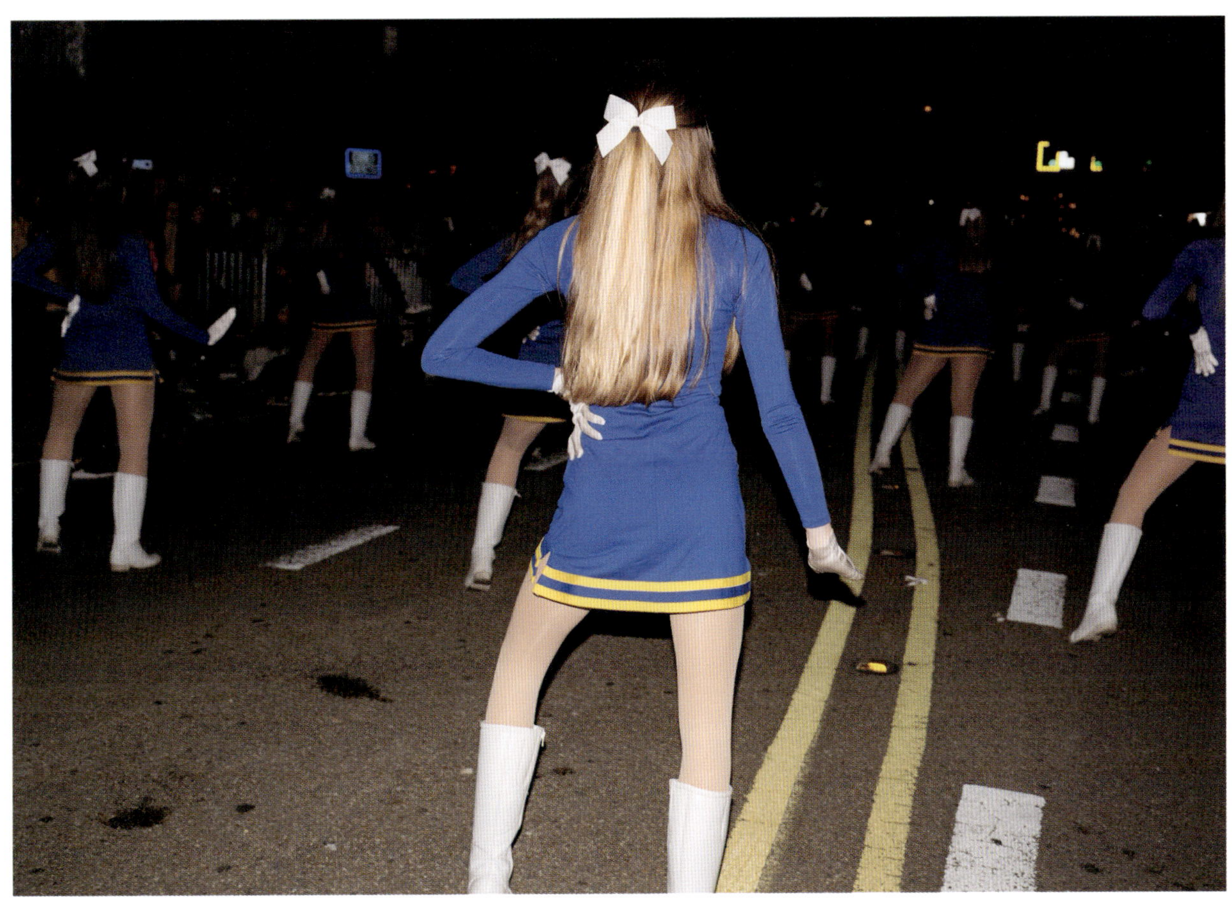

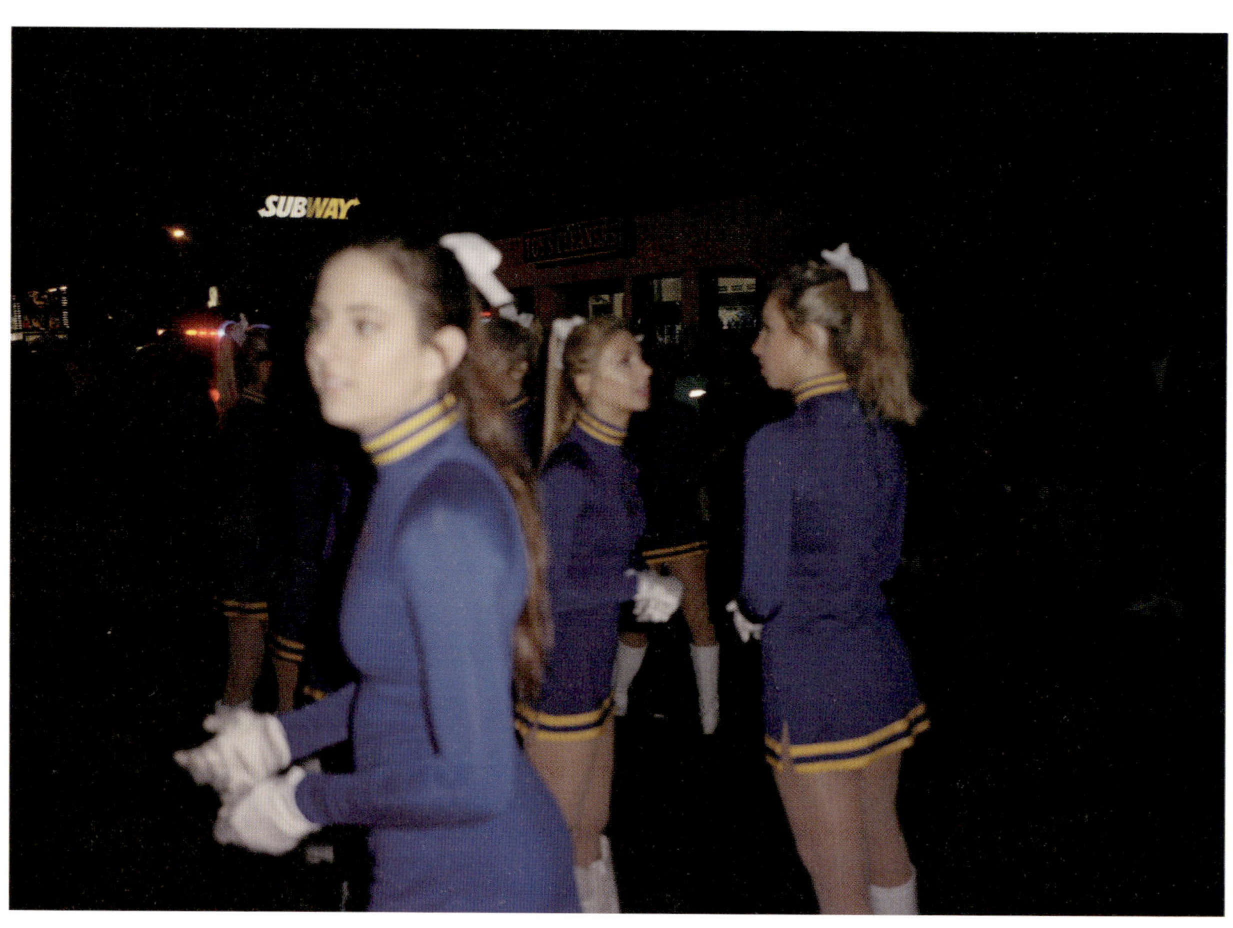

SUBWAY

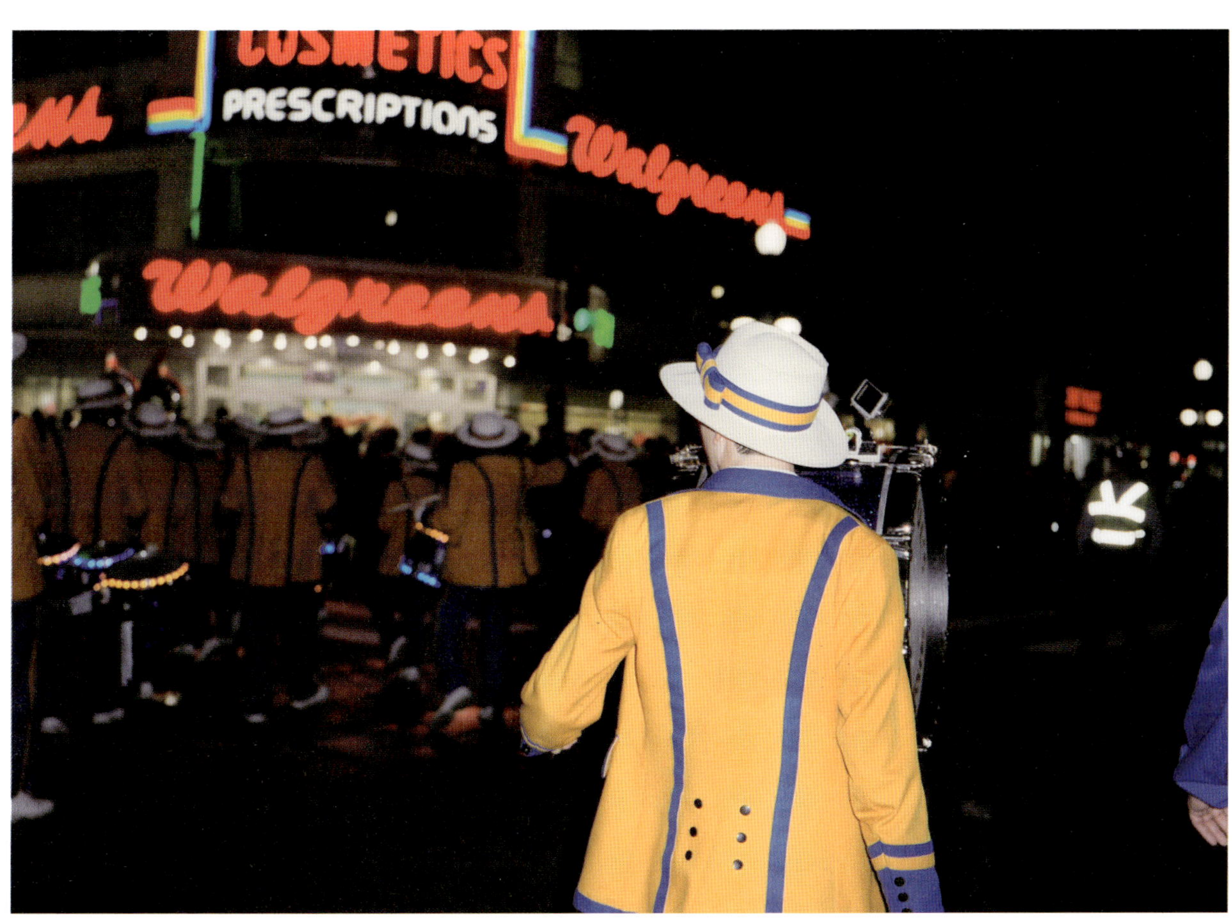
COSMETICS
PRESCRIPTIONS
Walgreens
Walgreens

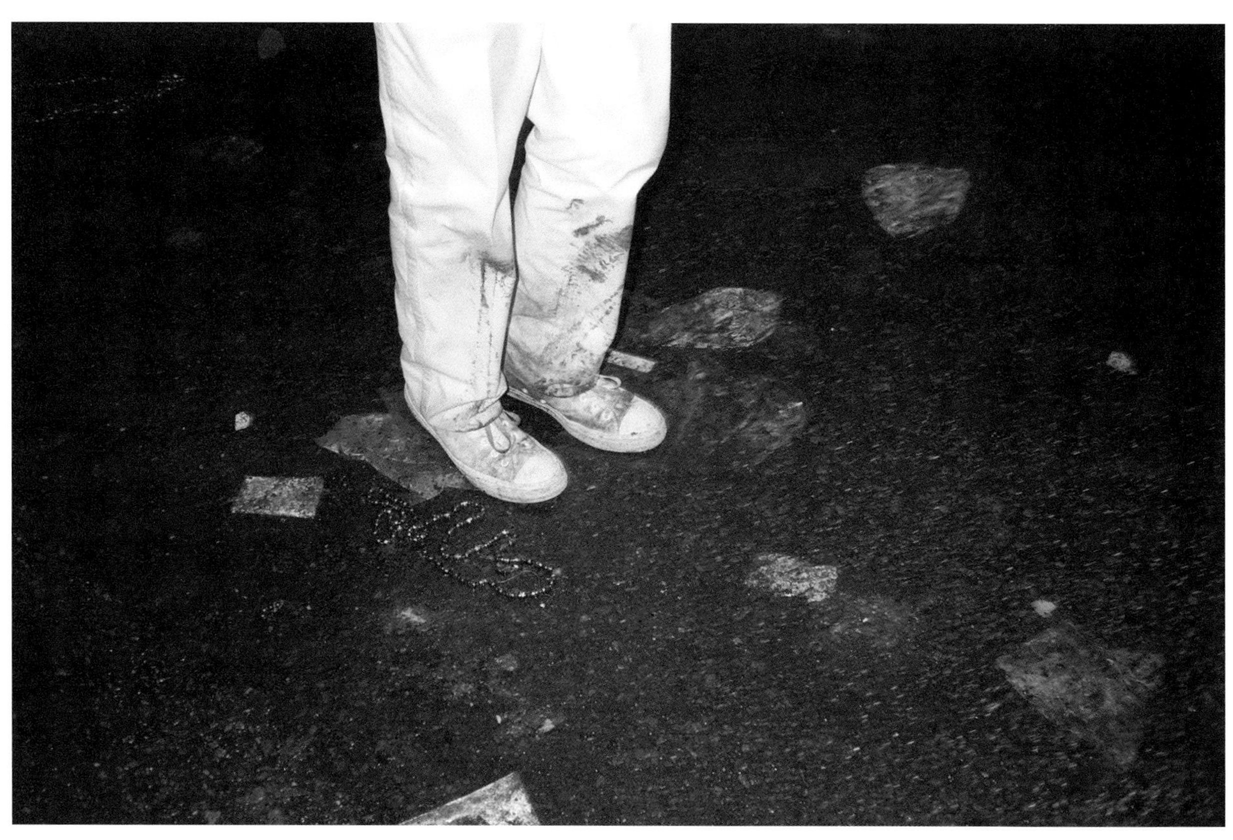

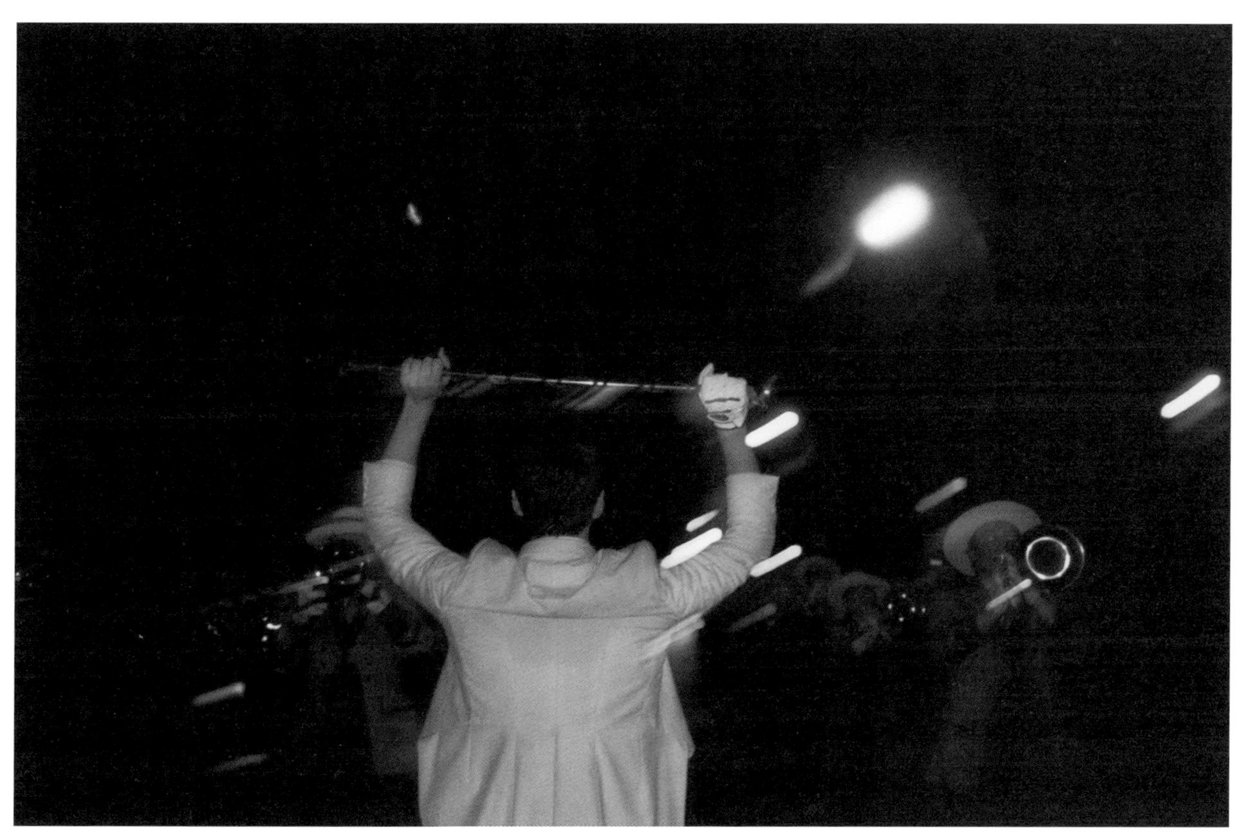

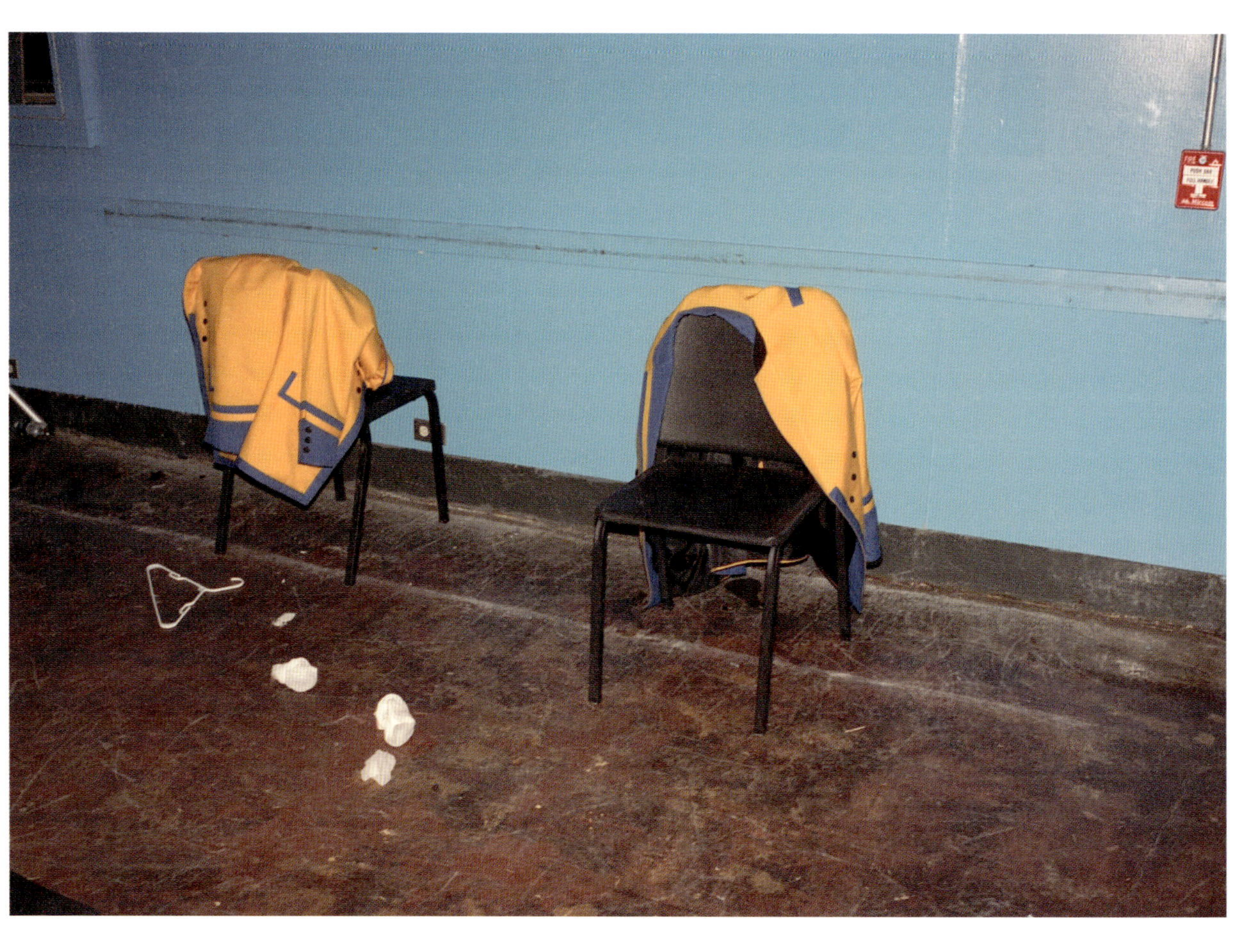

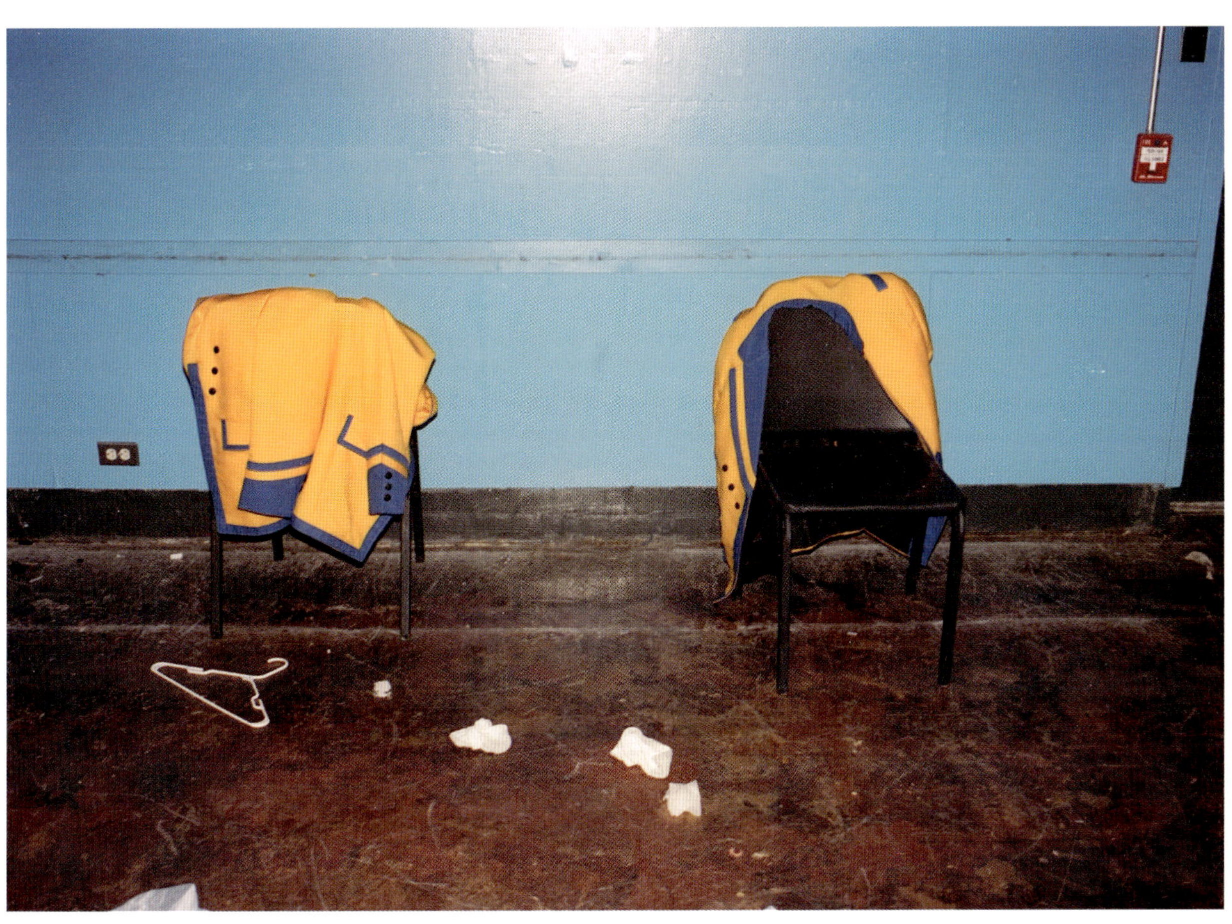

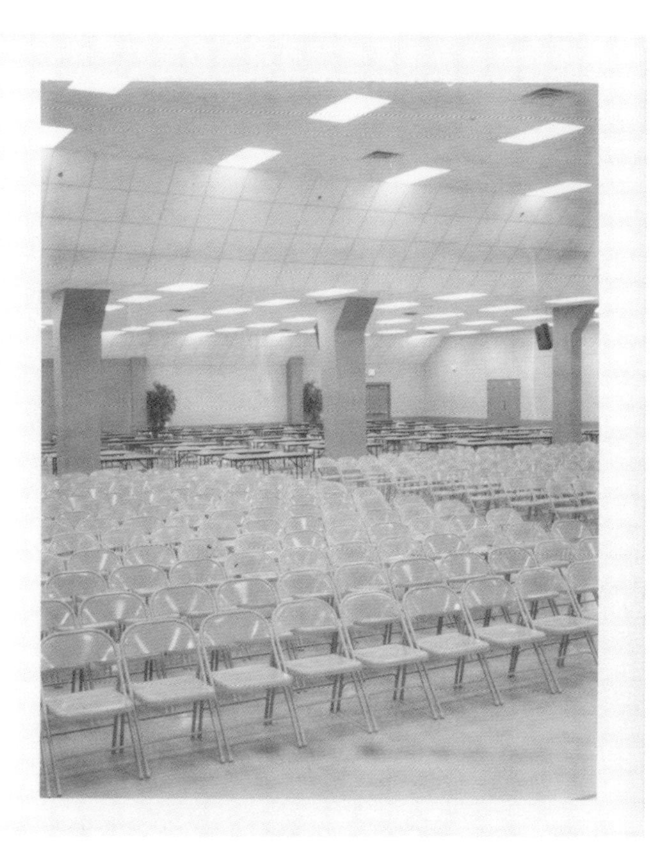

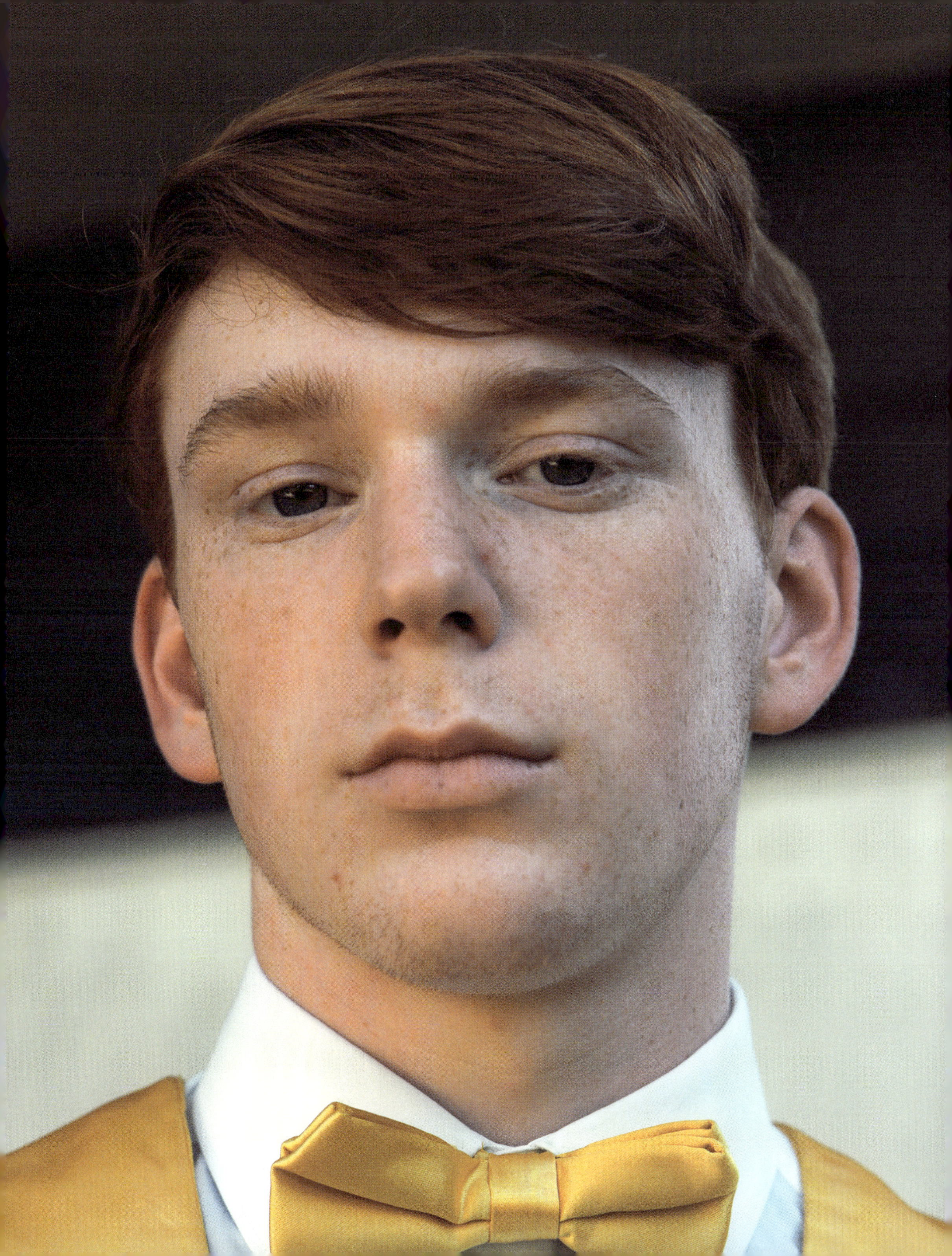

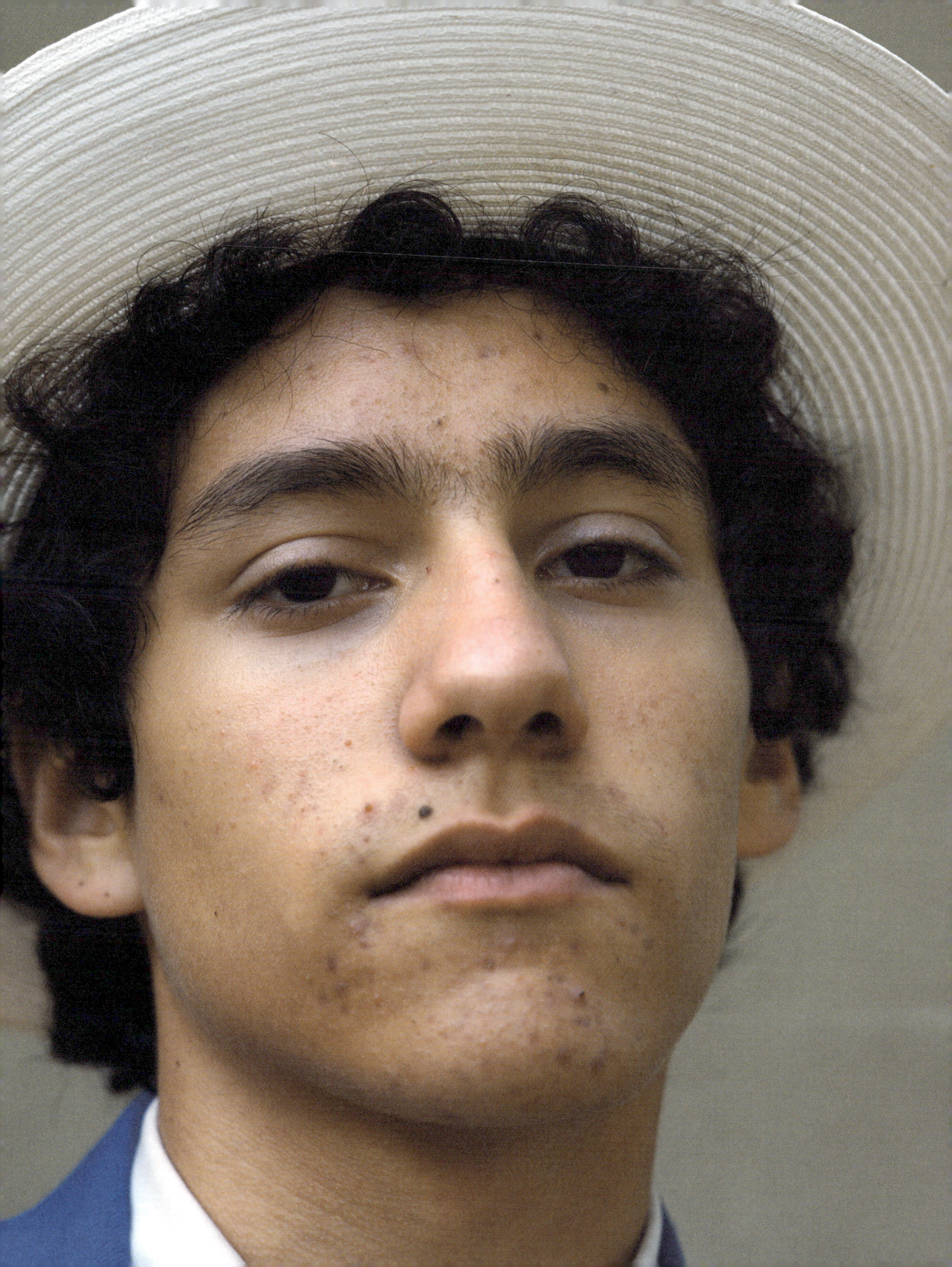

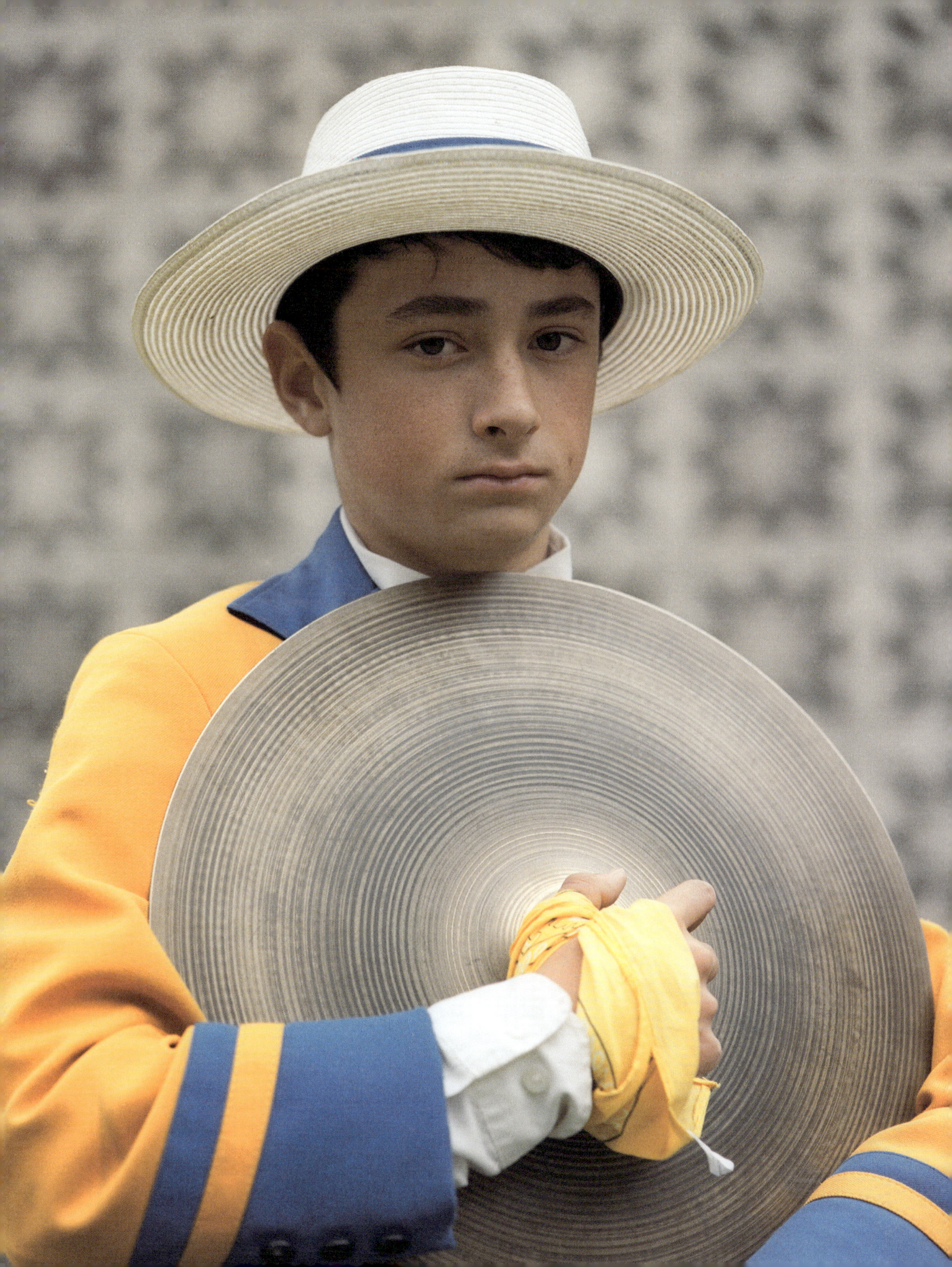

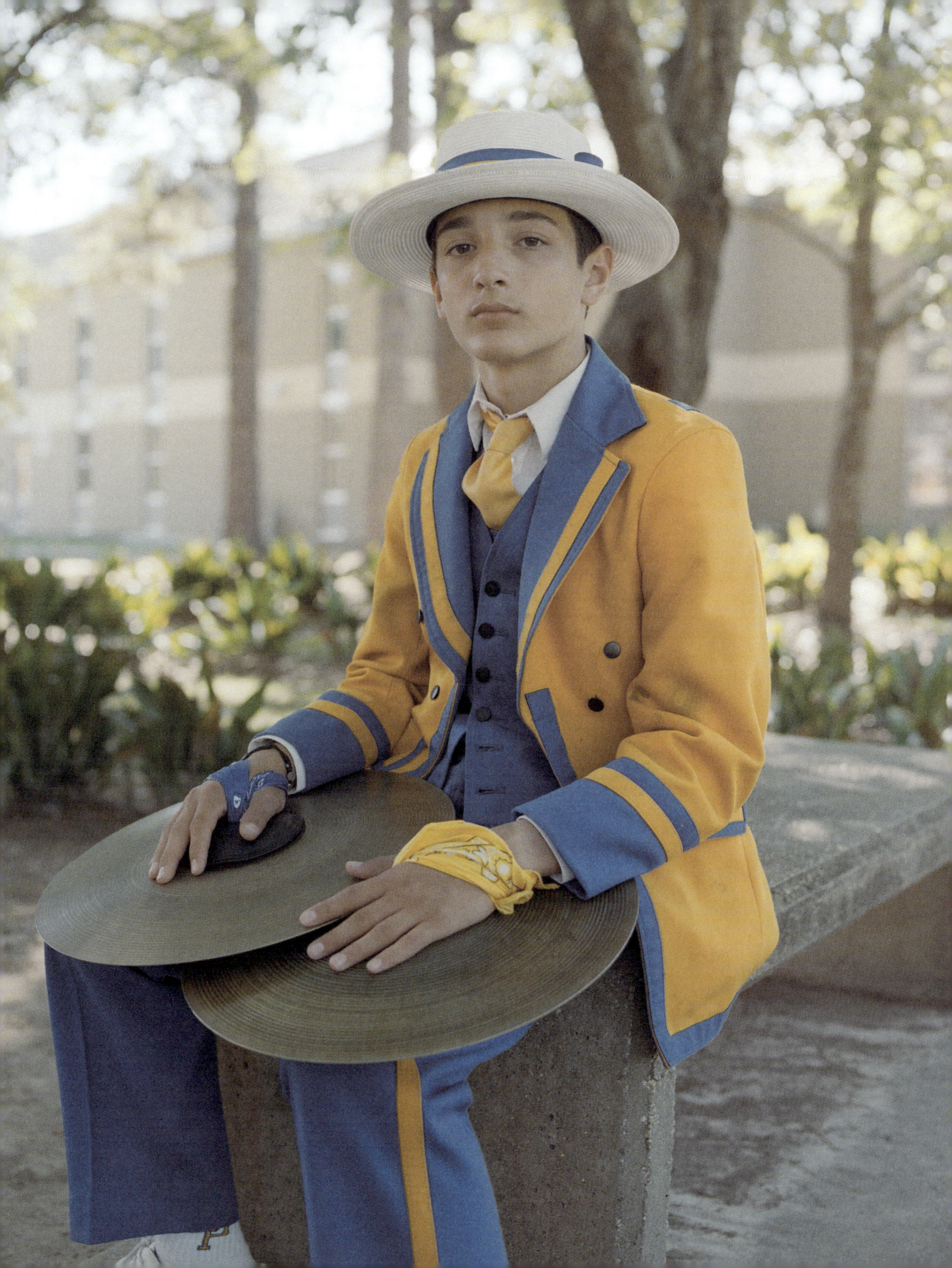

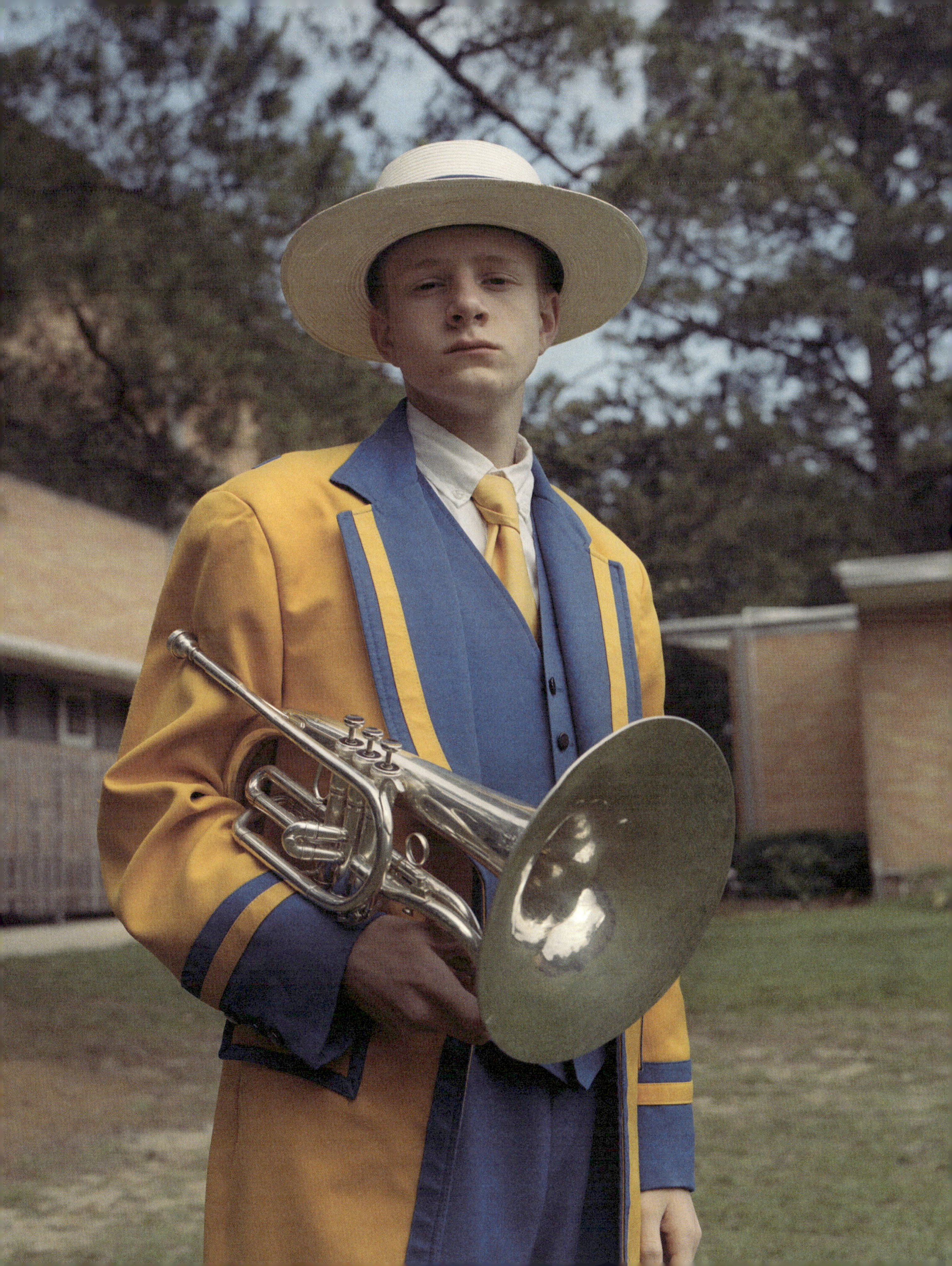

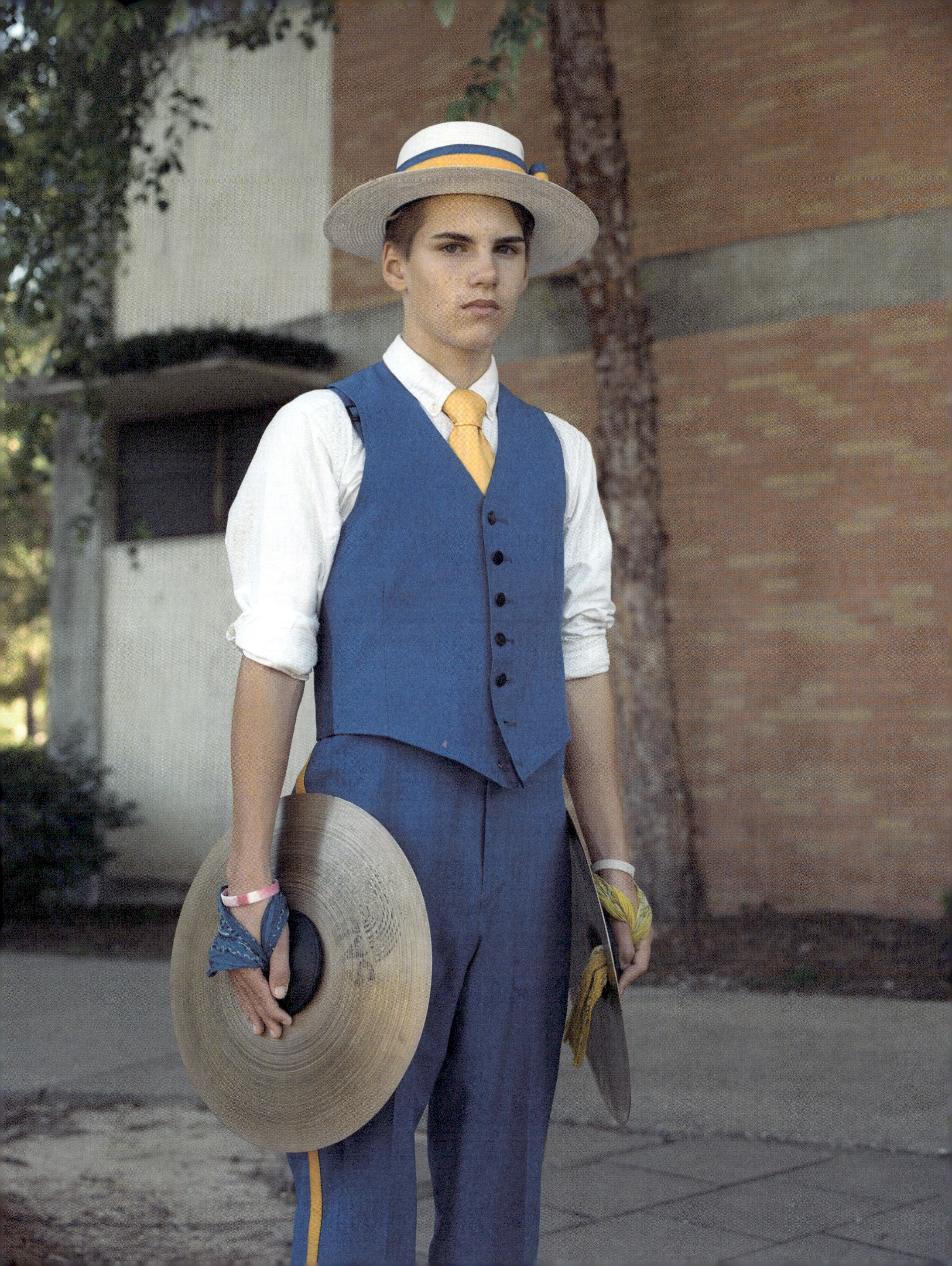

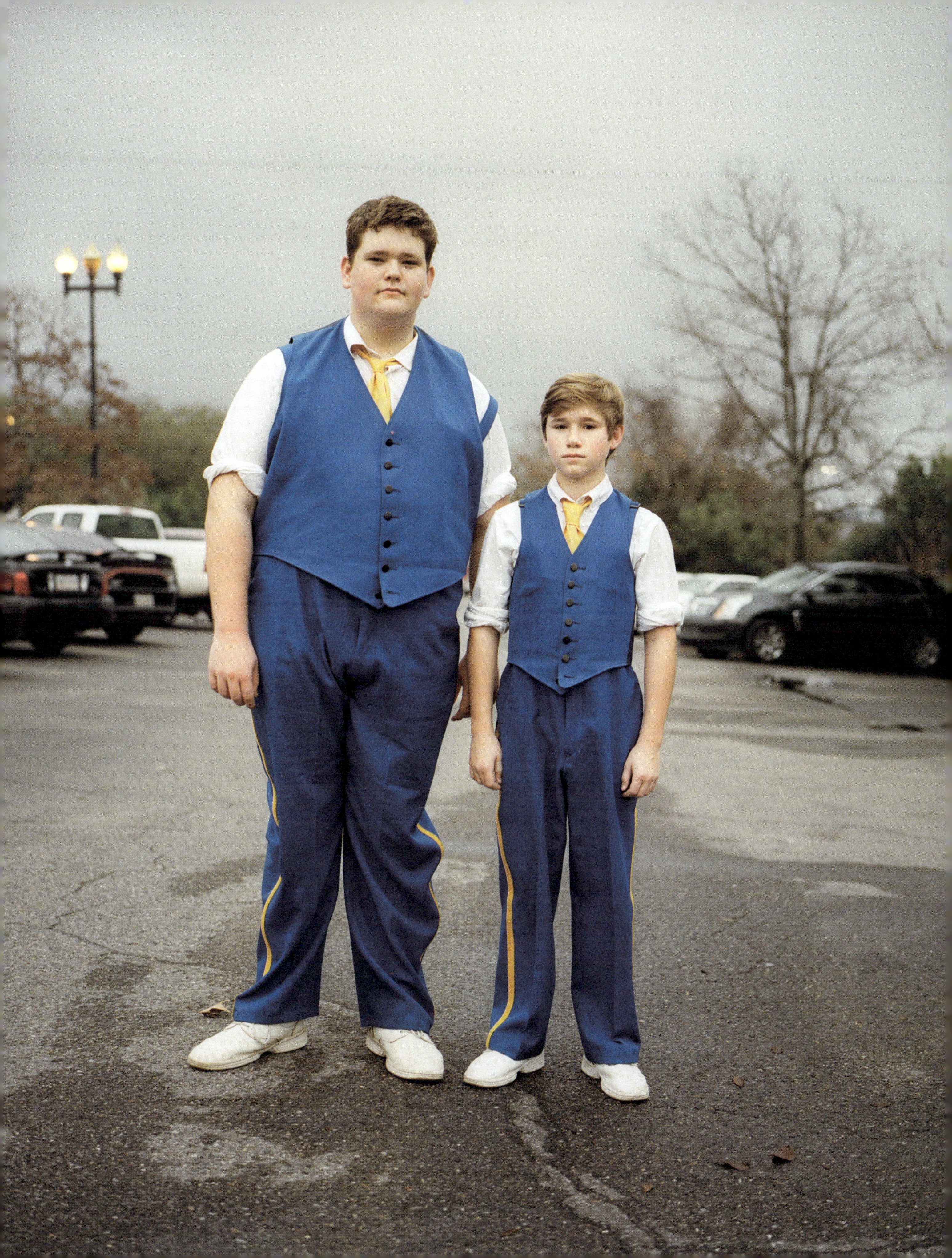

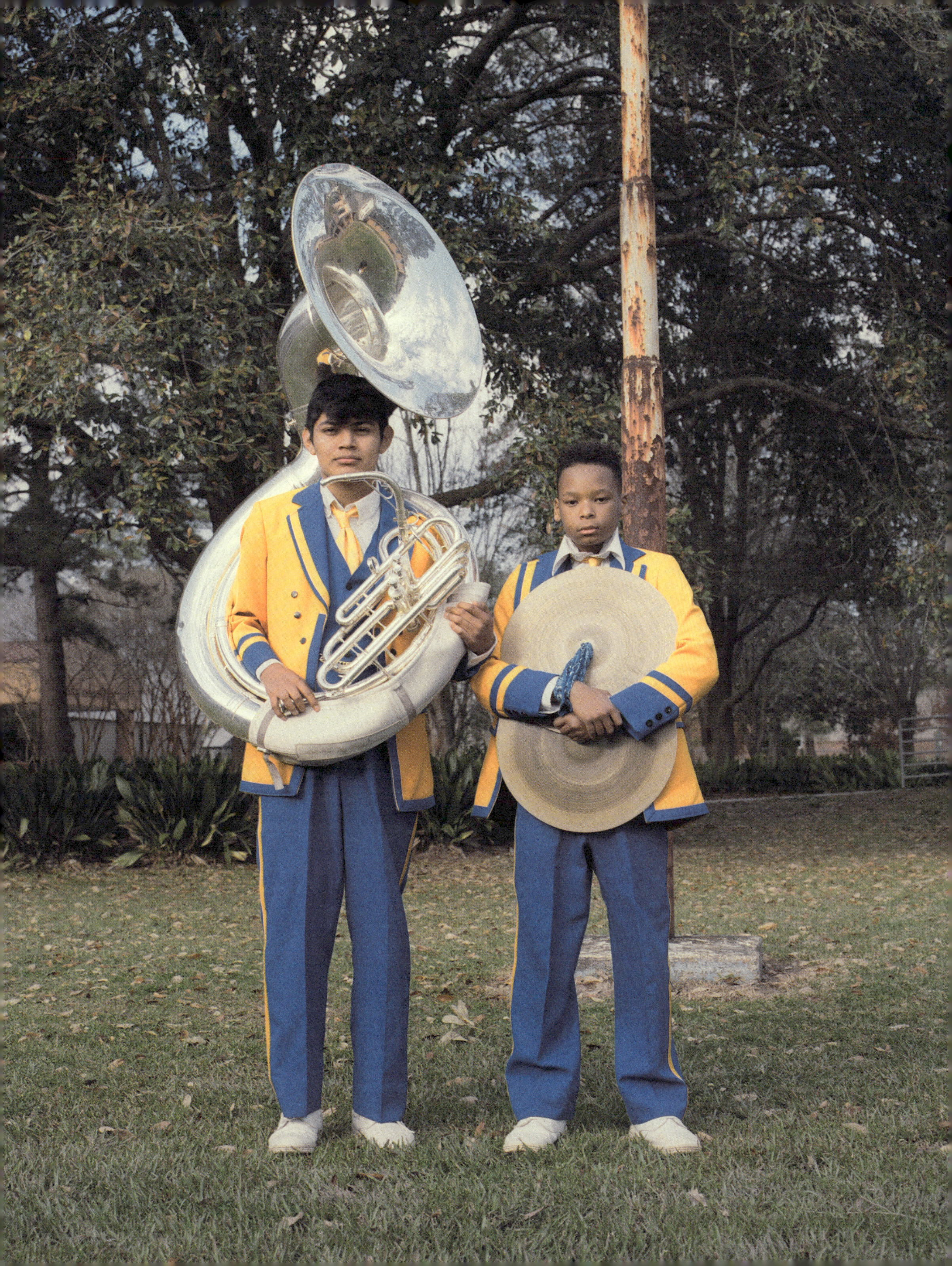

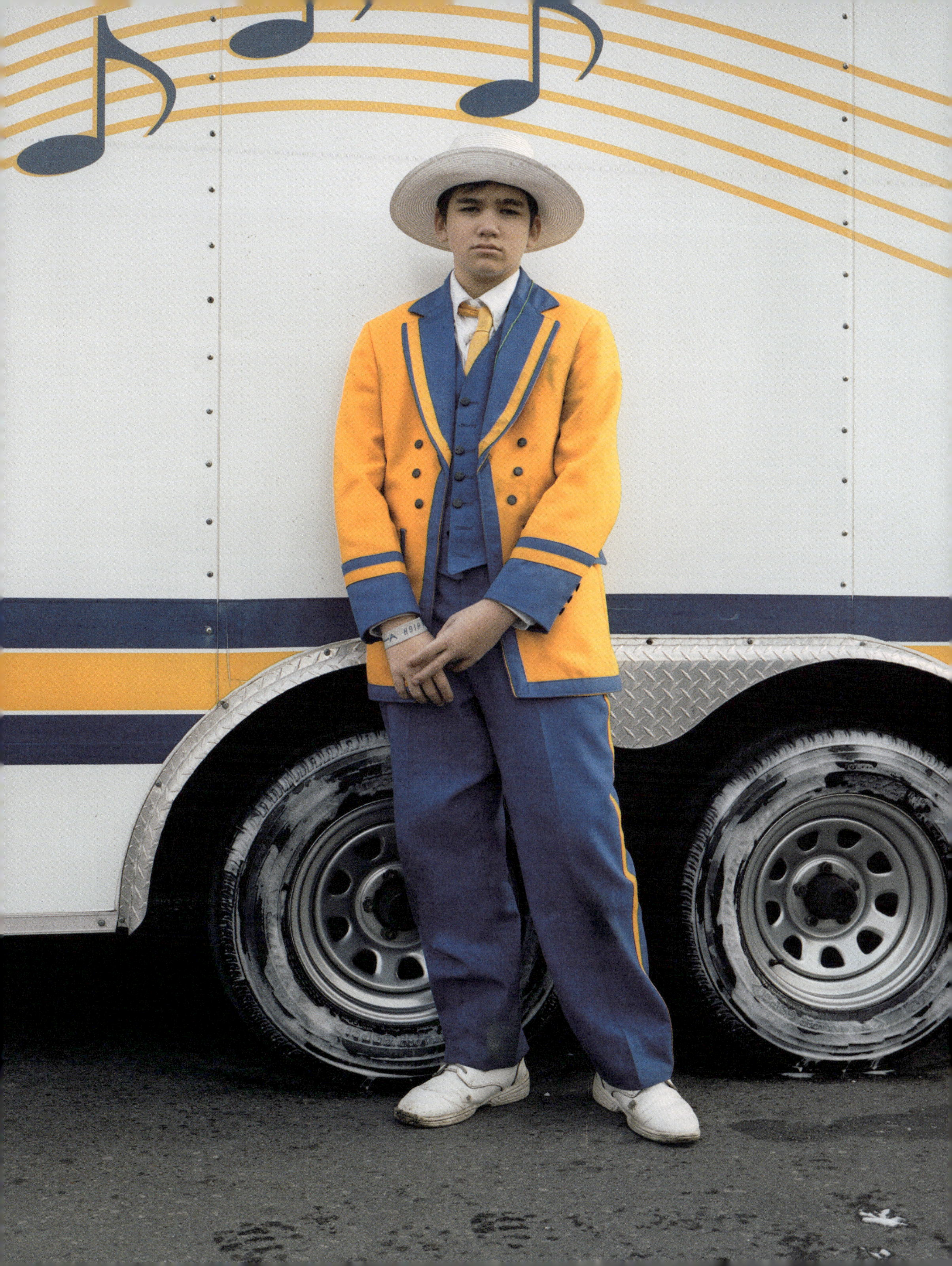

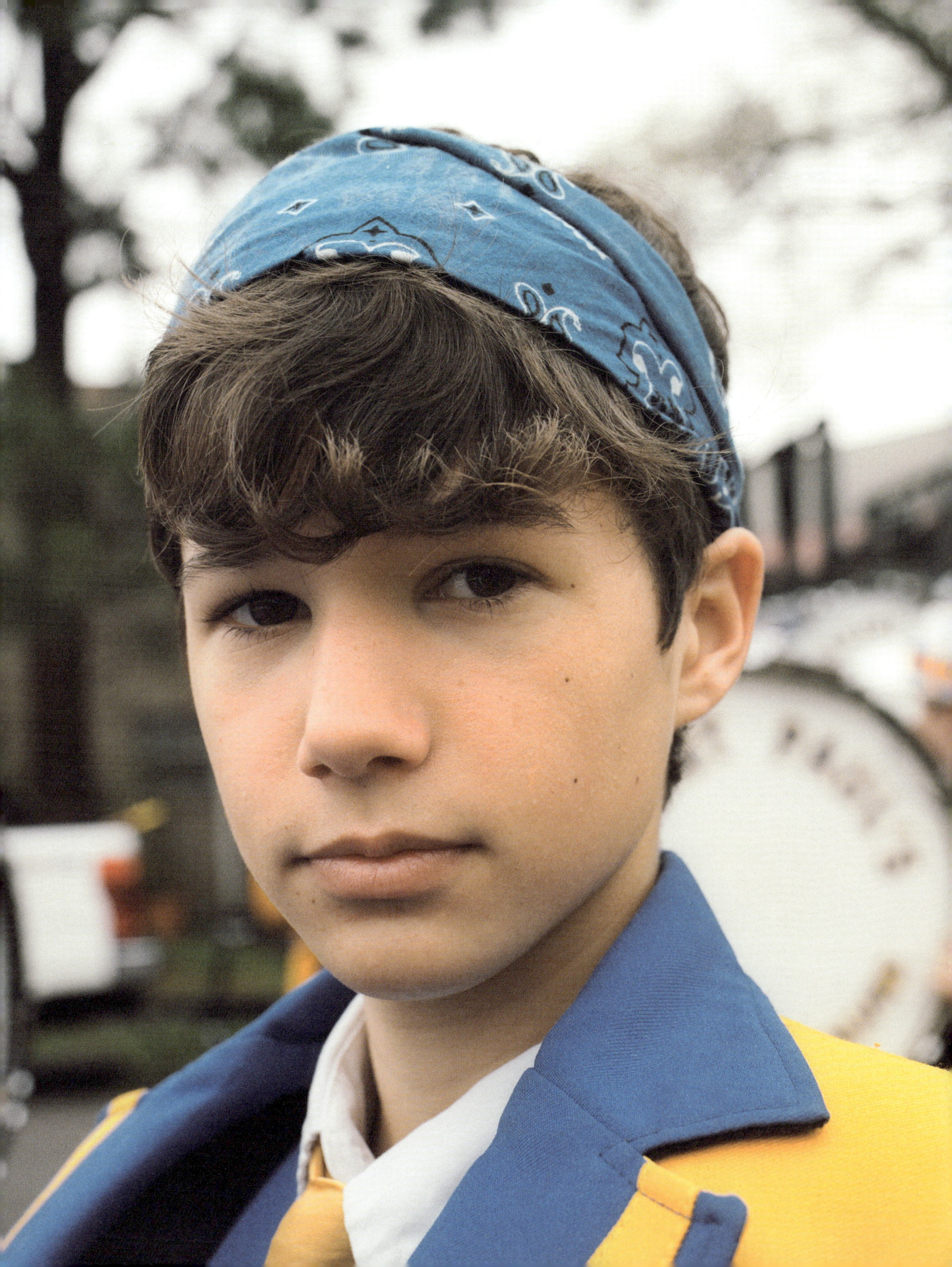

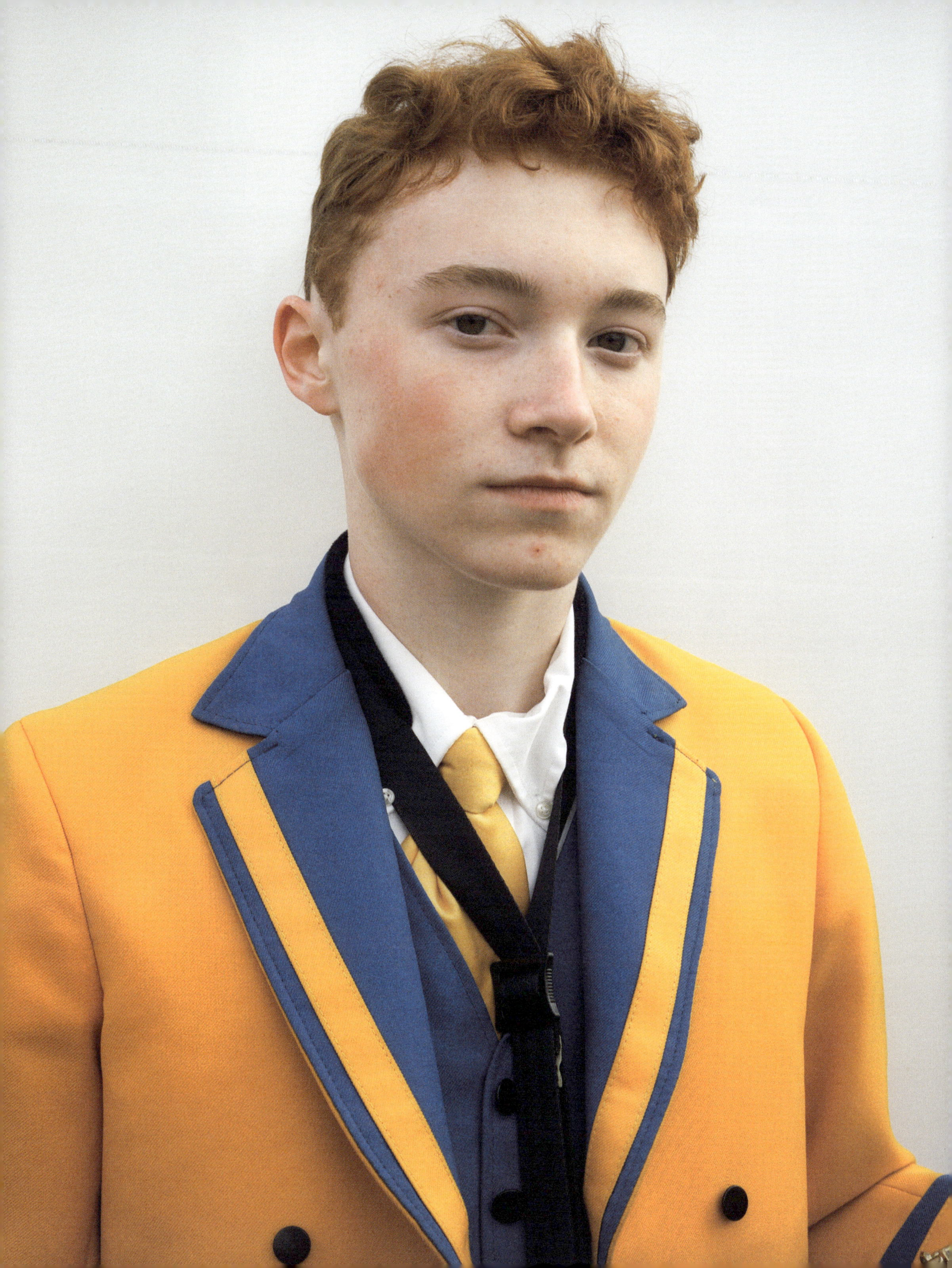

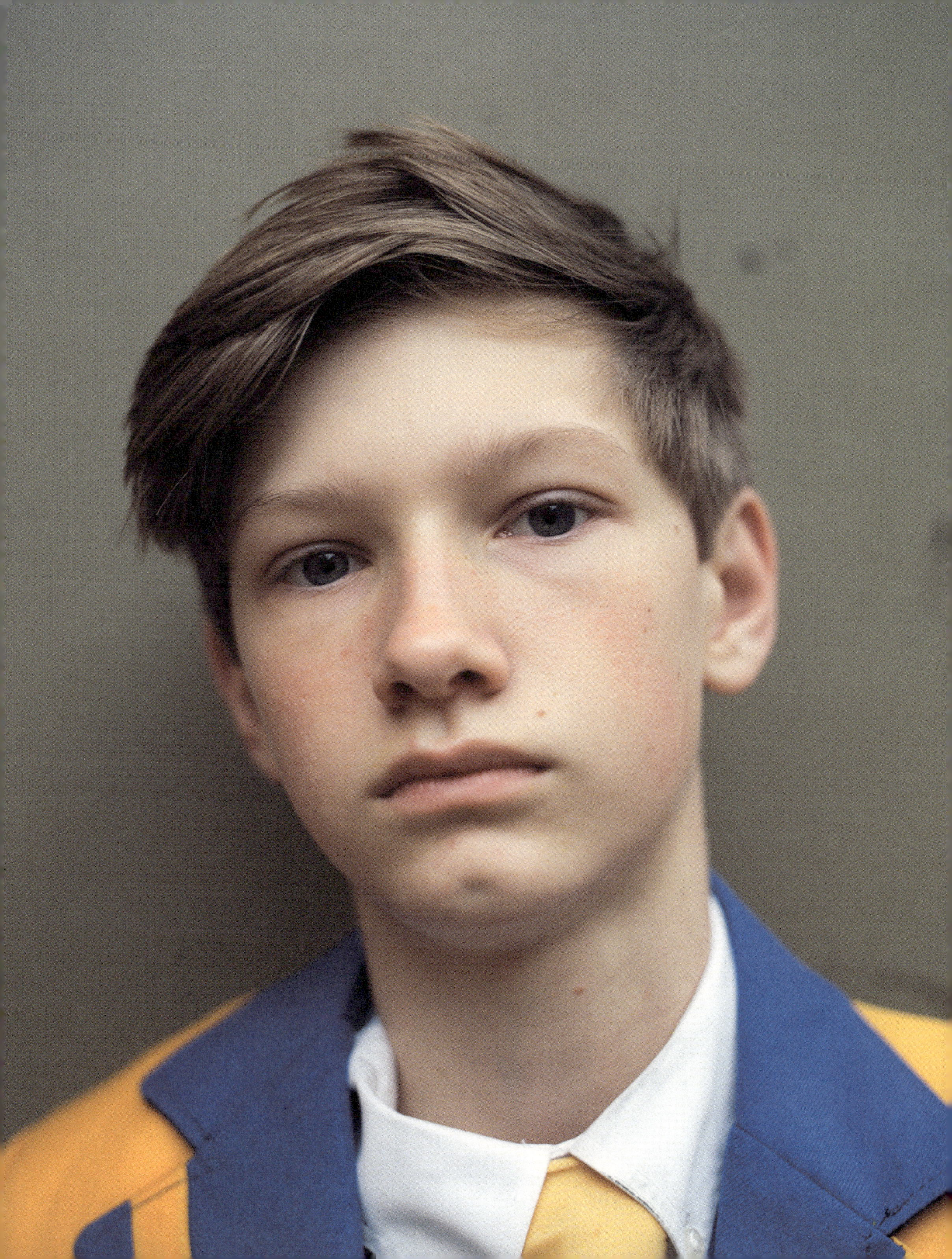

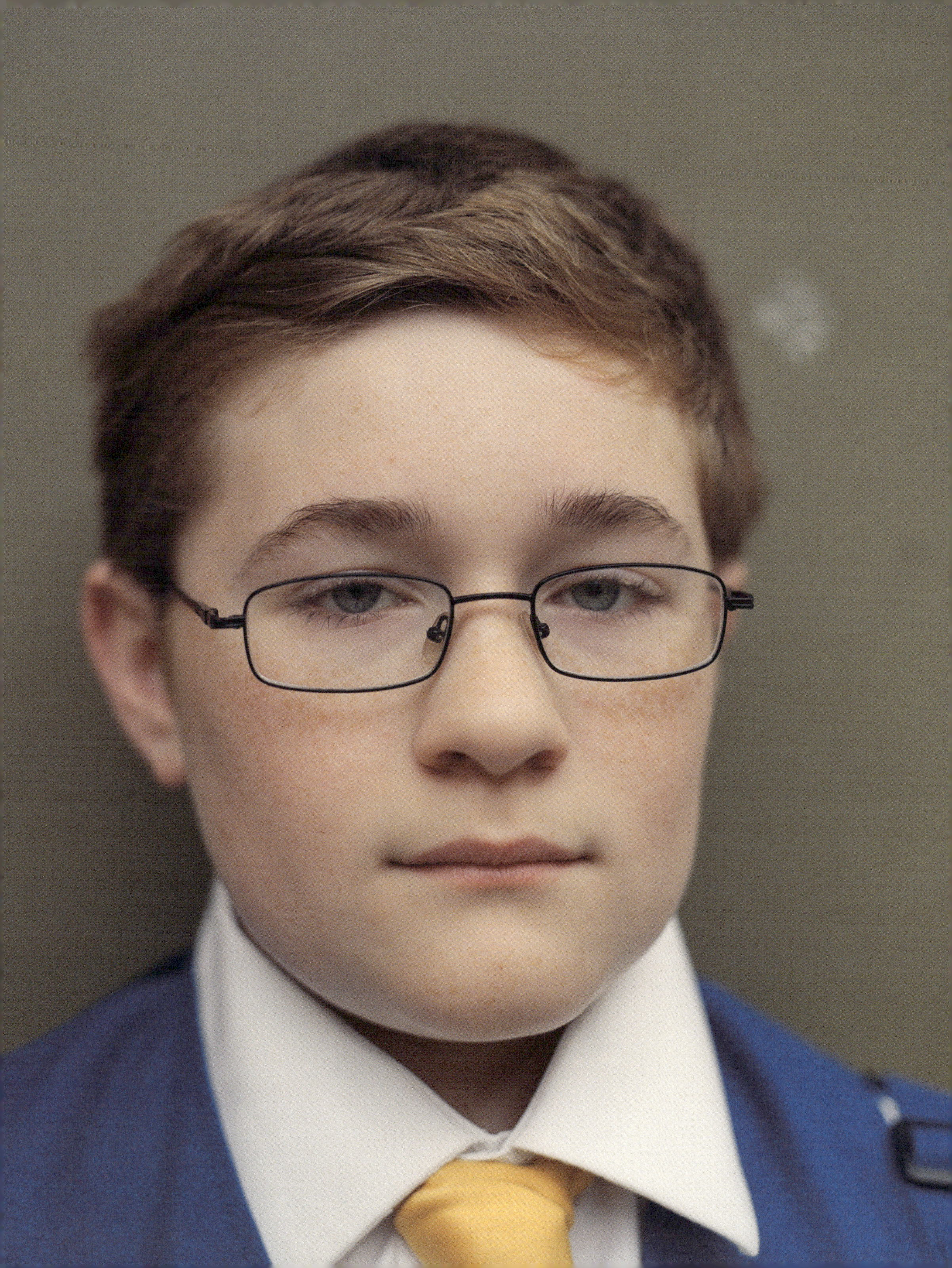

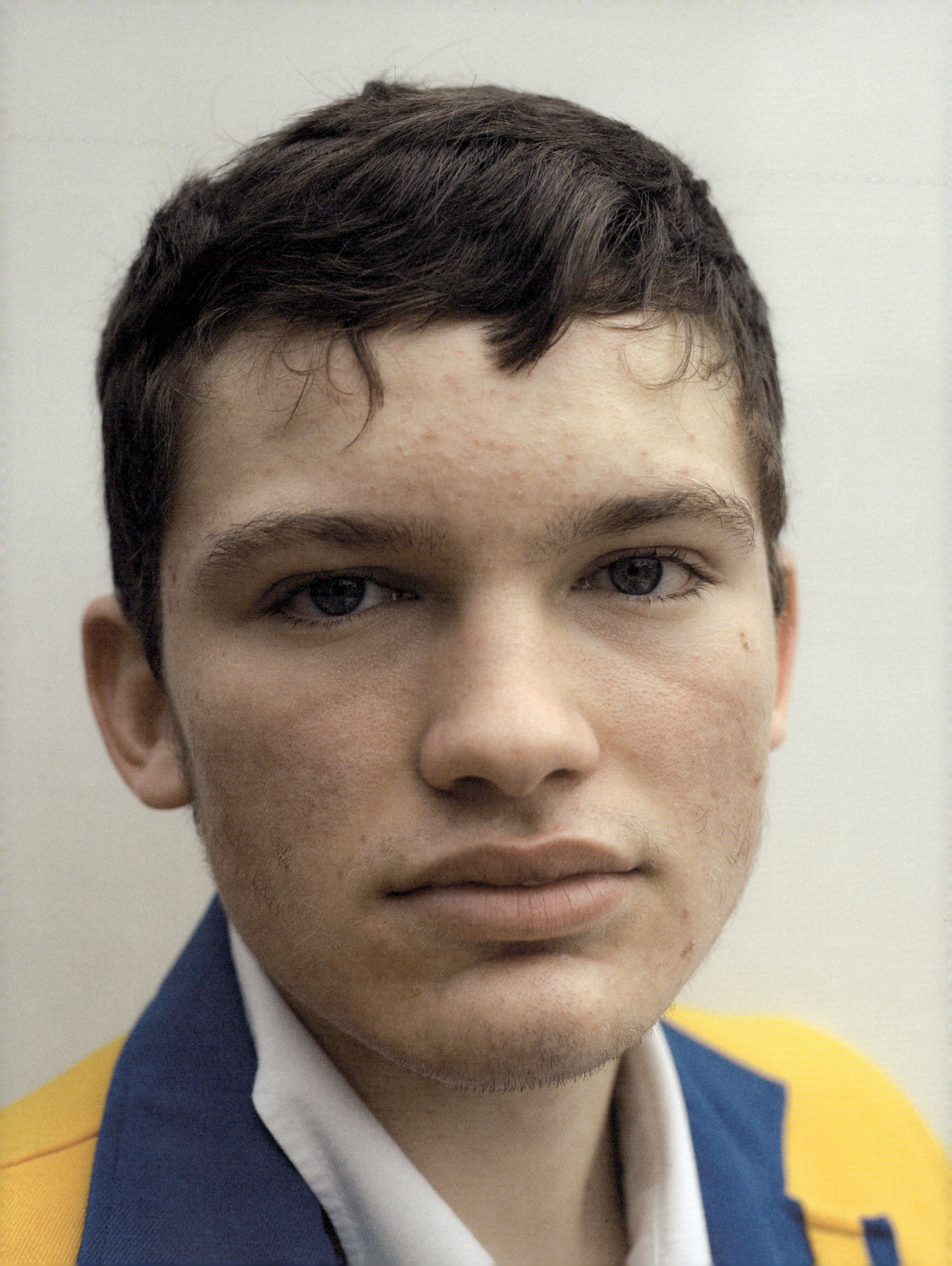

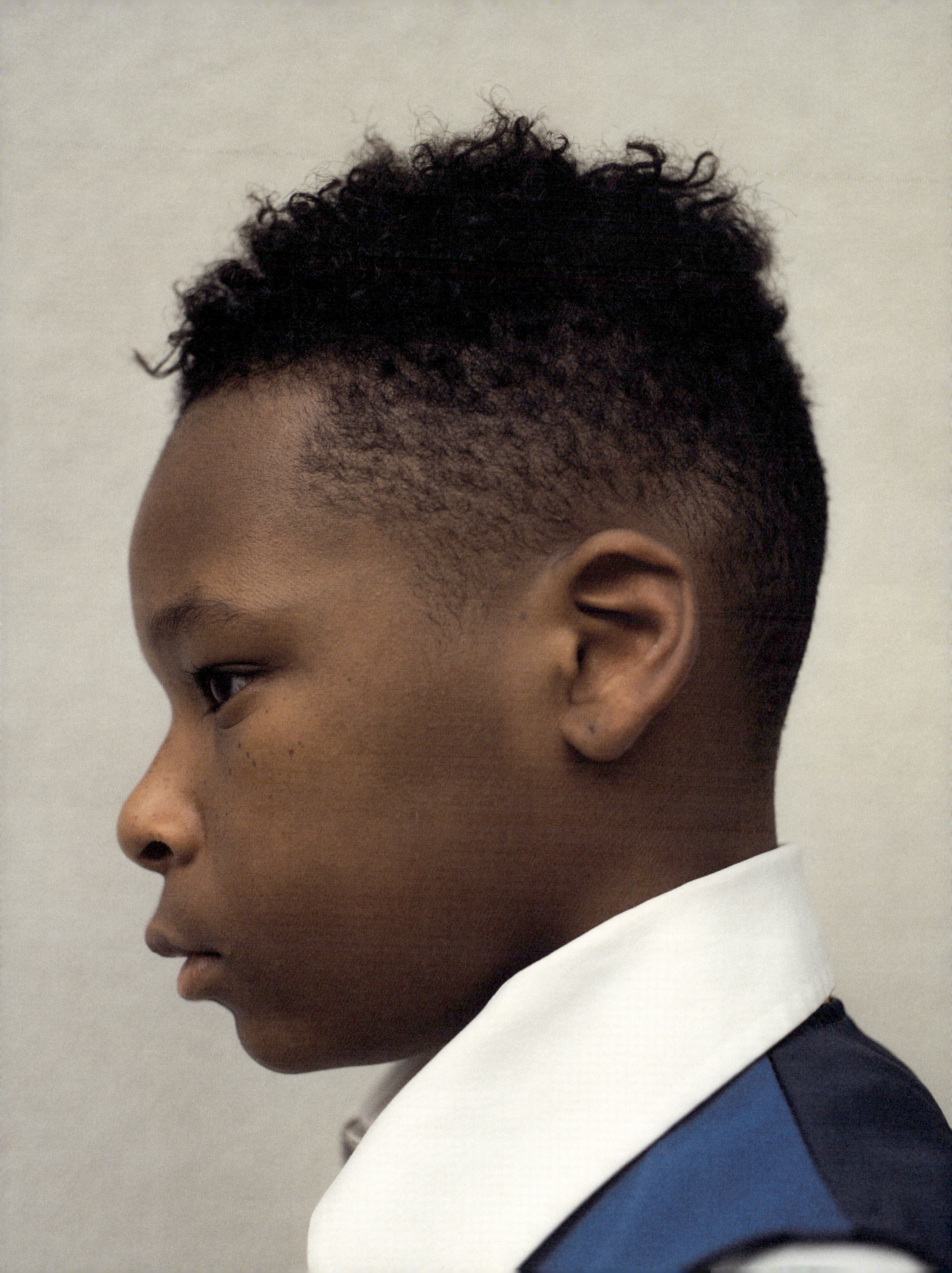

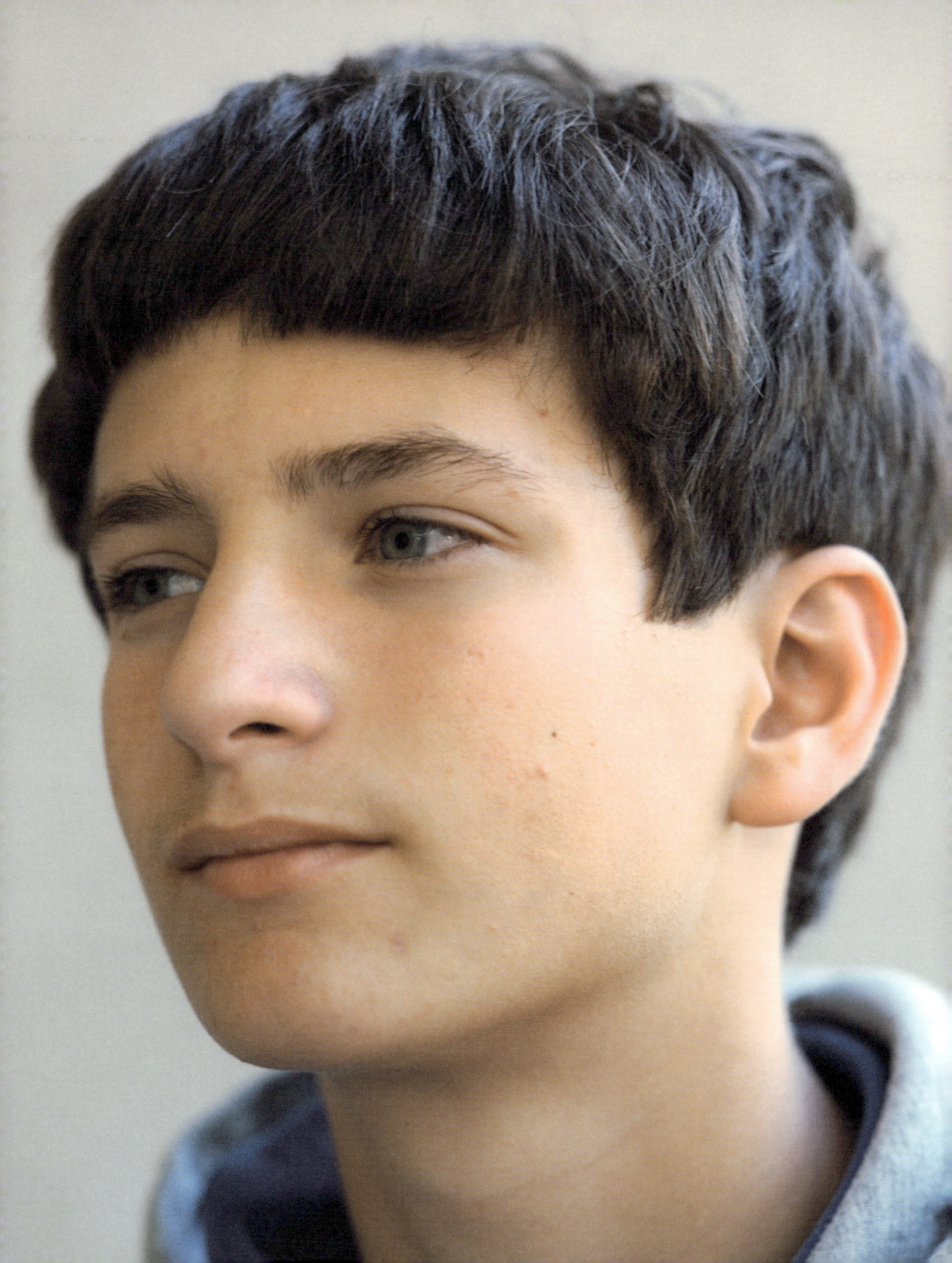

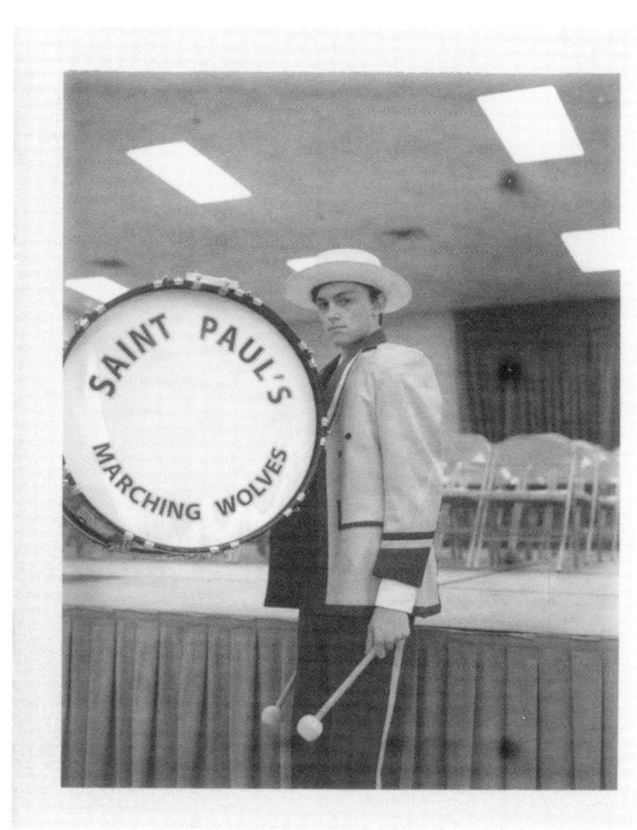

SAINT PAUL'S
MARCHING WOLVES

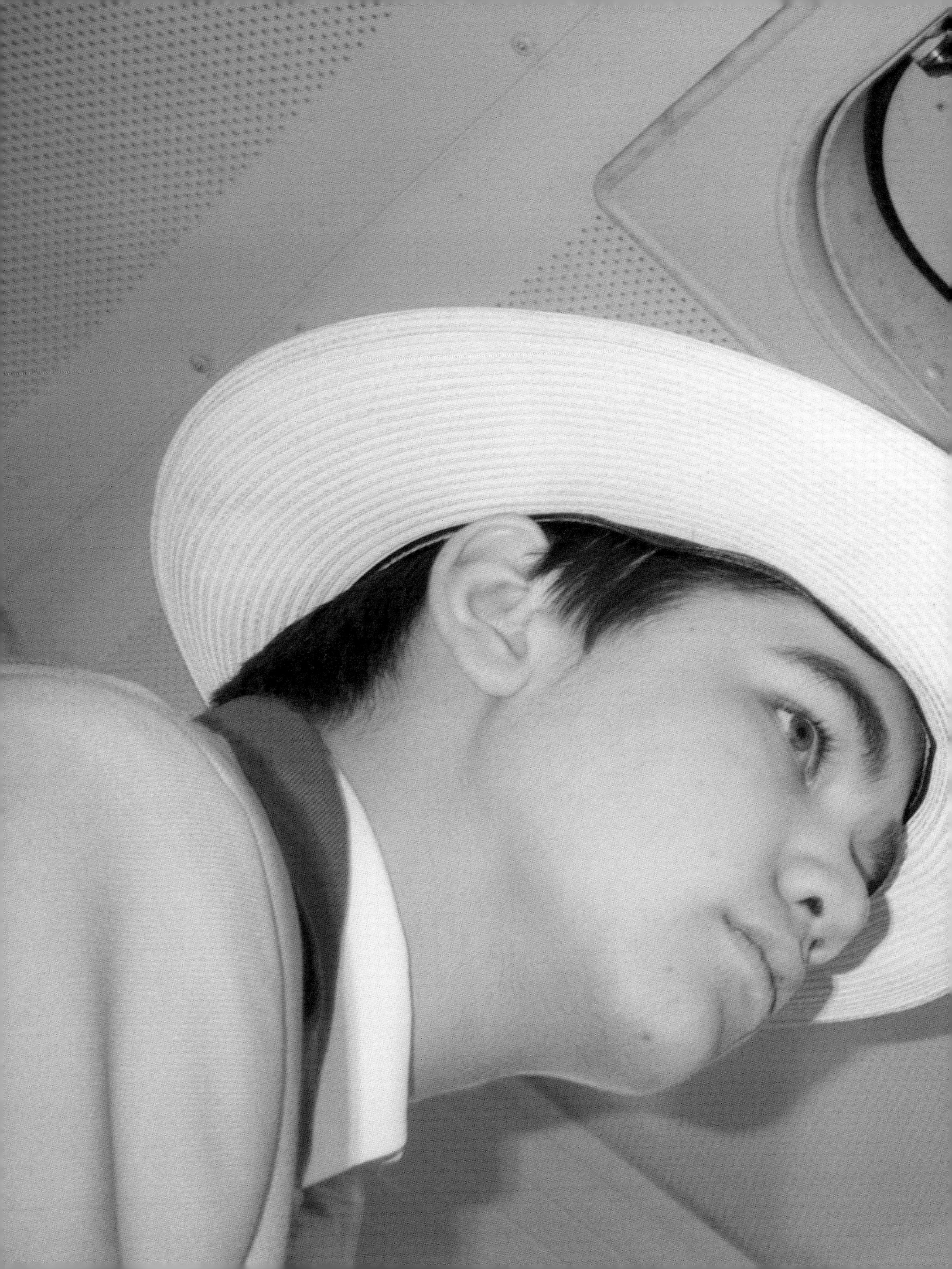

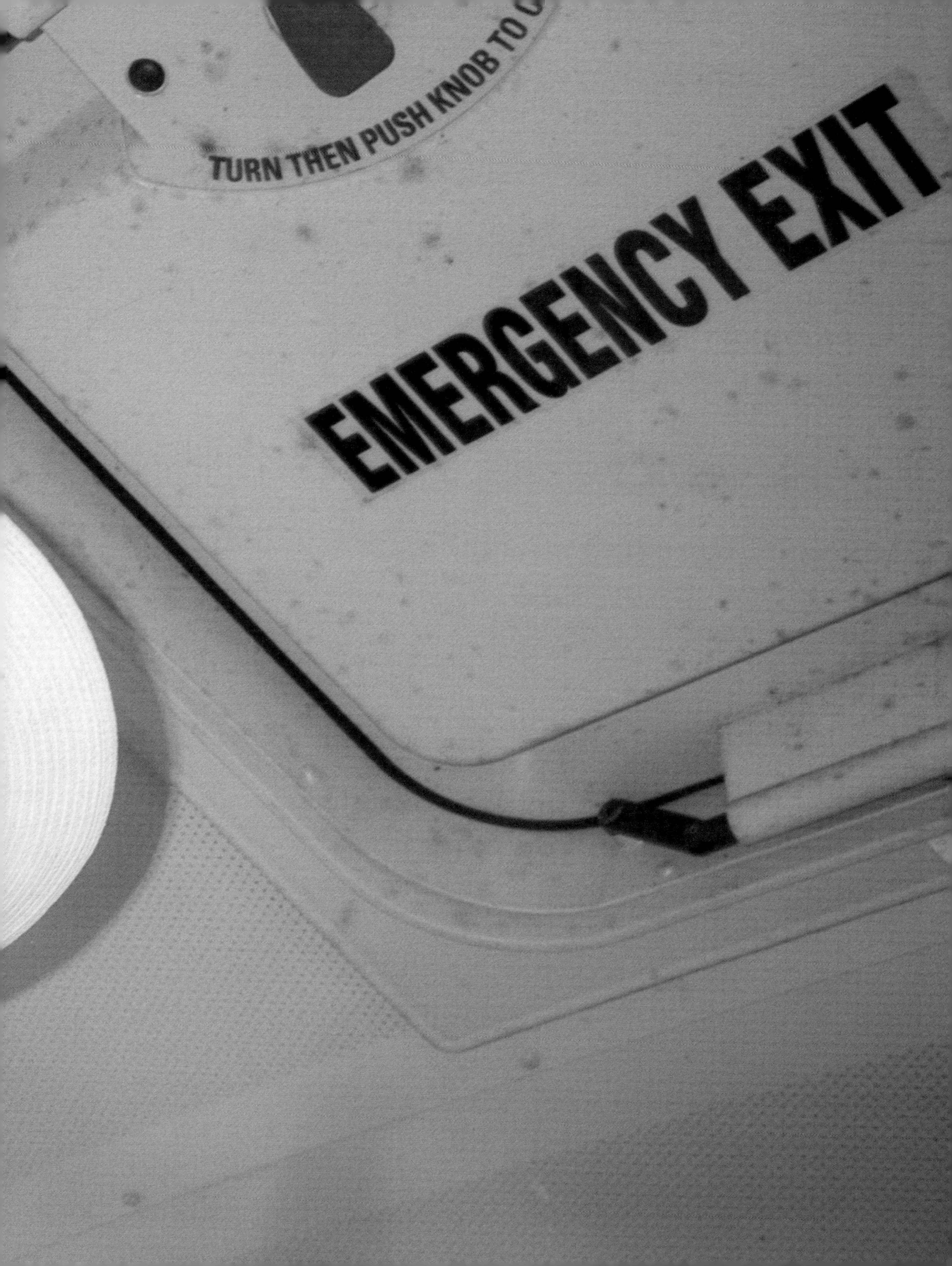

TURN THEN PUSH KNOB TO O
EMERGENCY EXIT

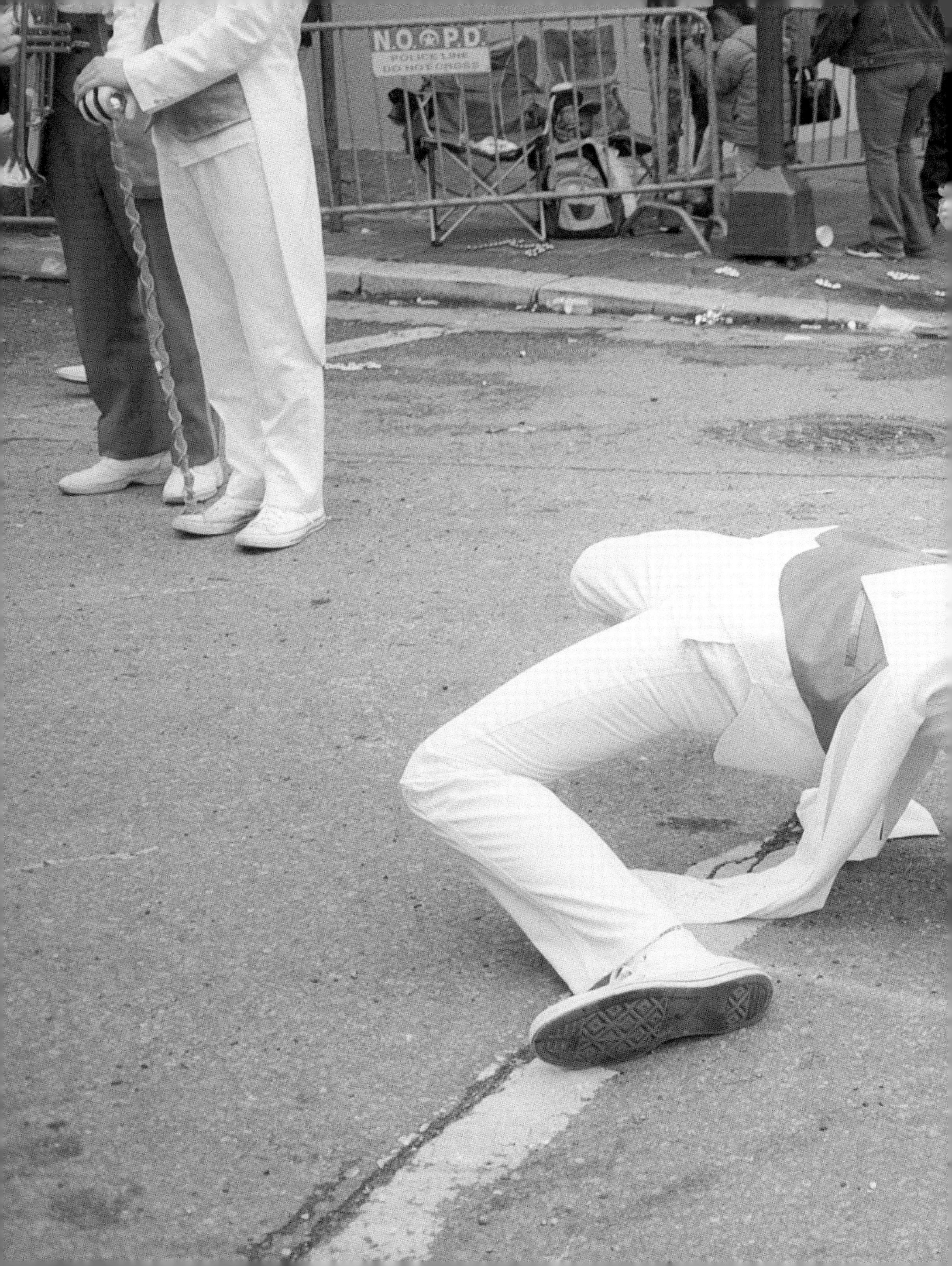

N.O.P.D.
POLICE LINE
DO NOT CROSS

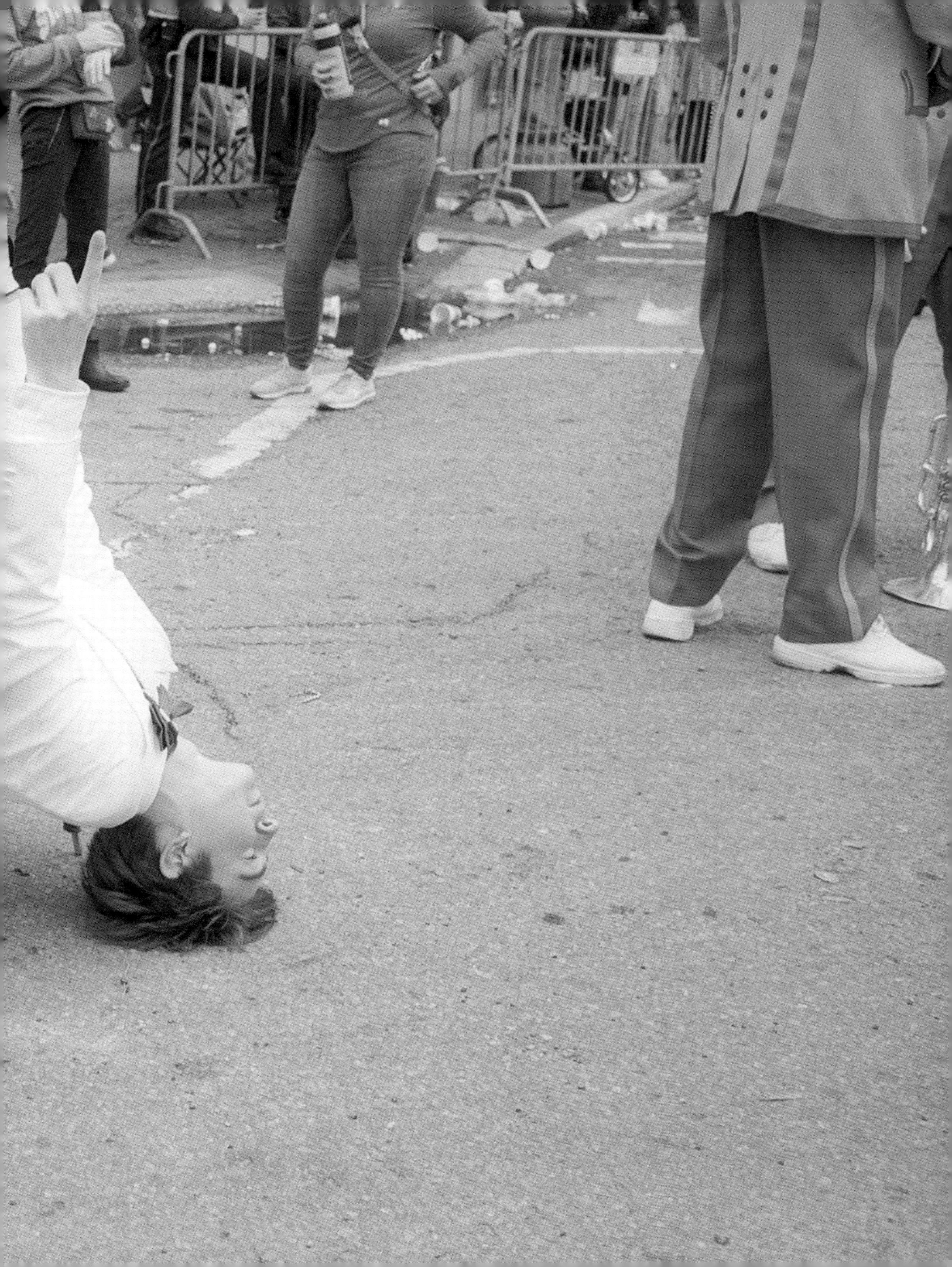

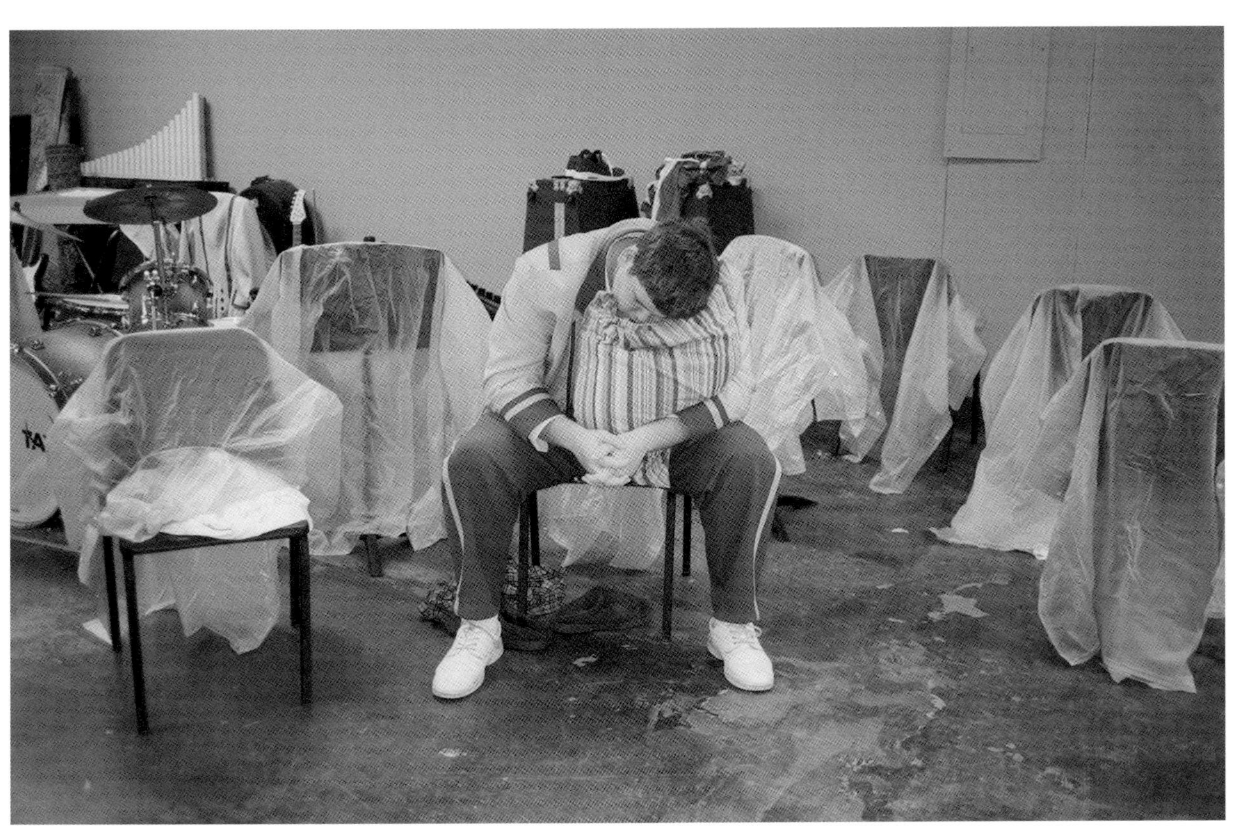

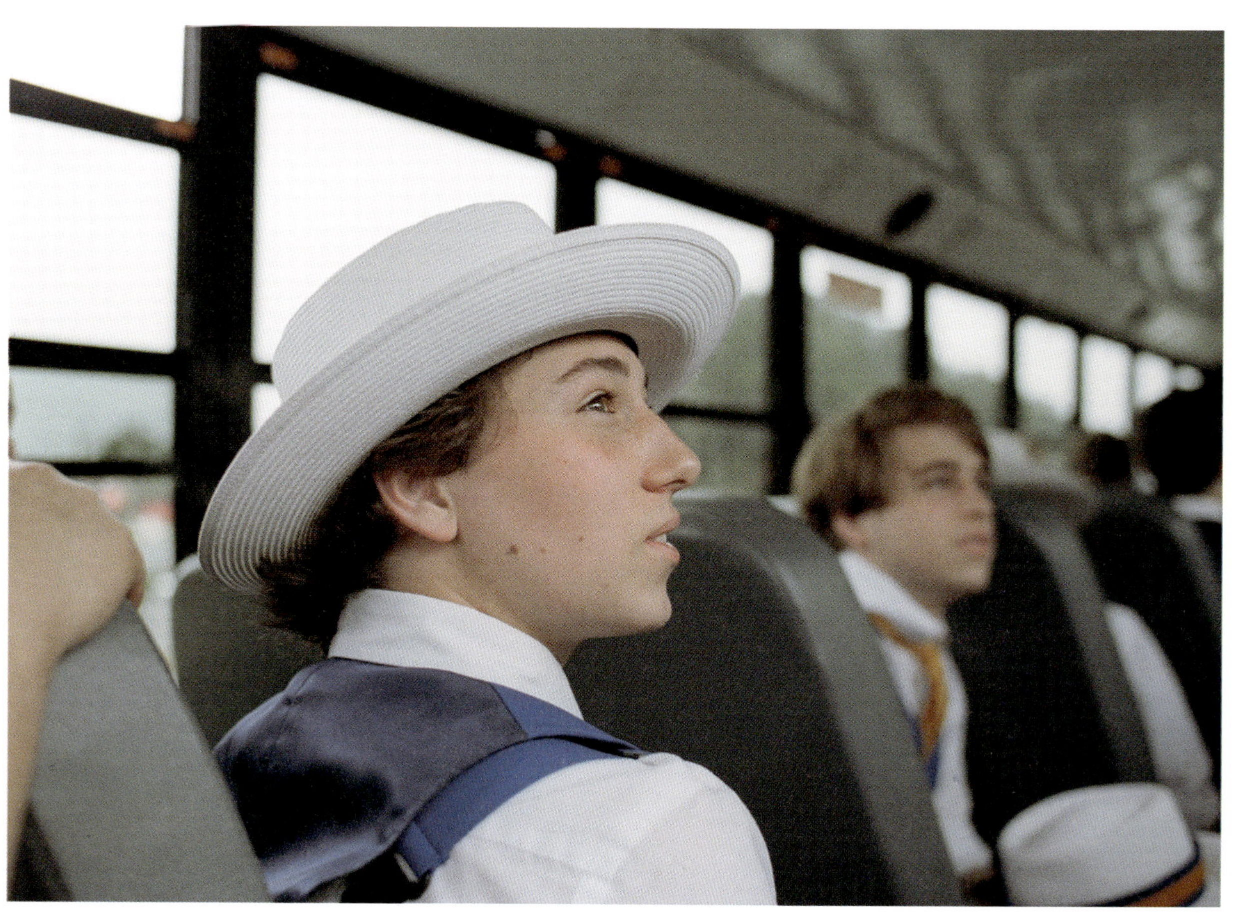

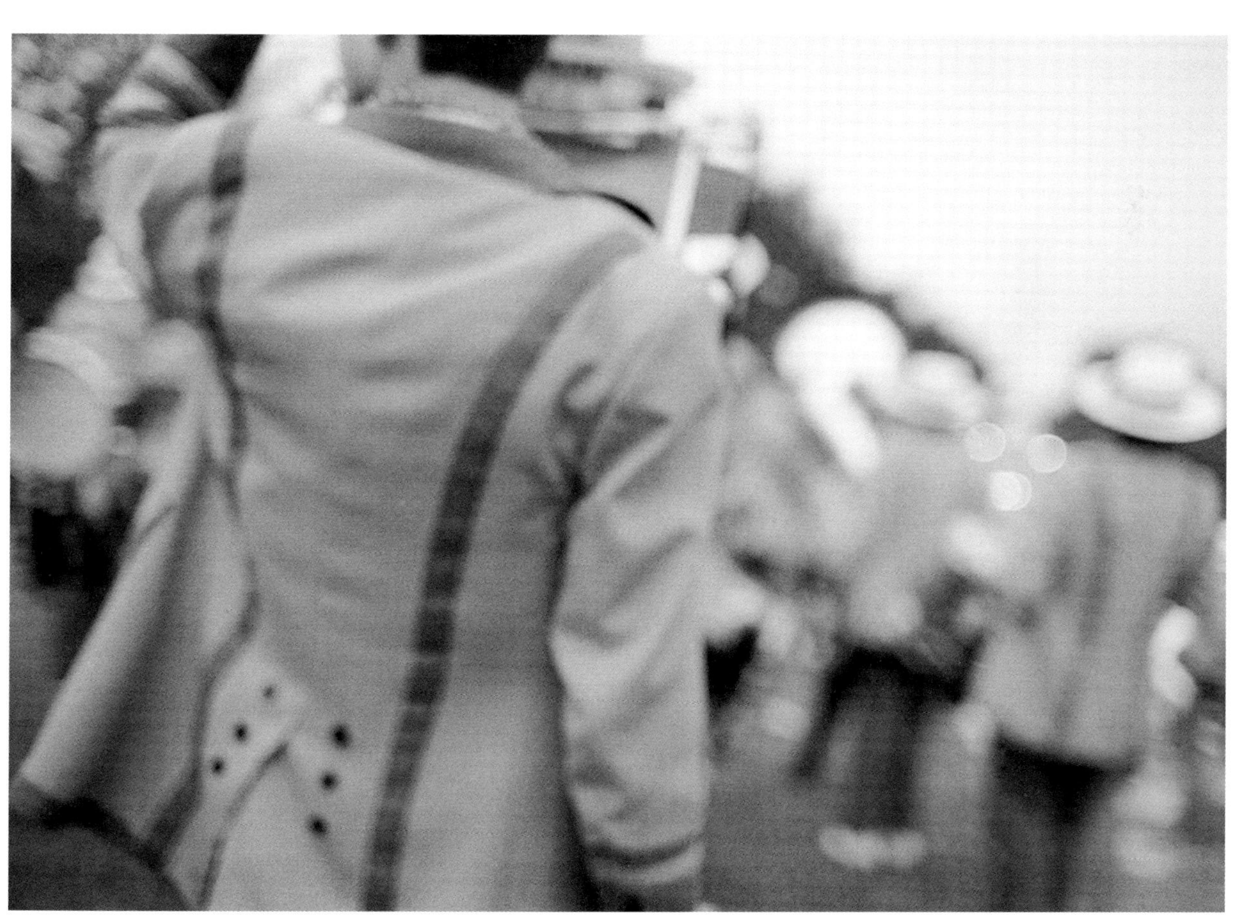

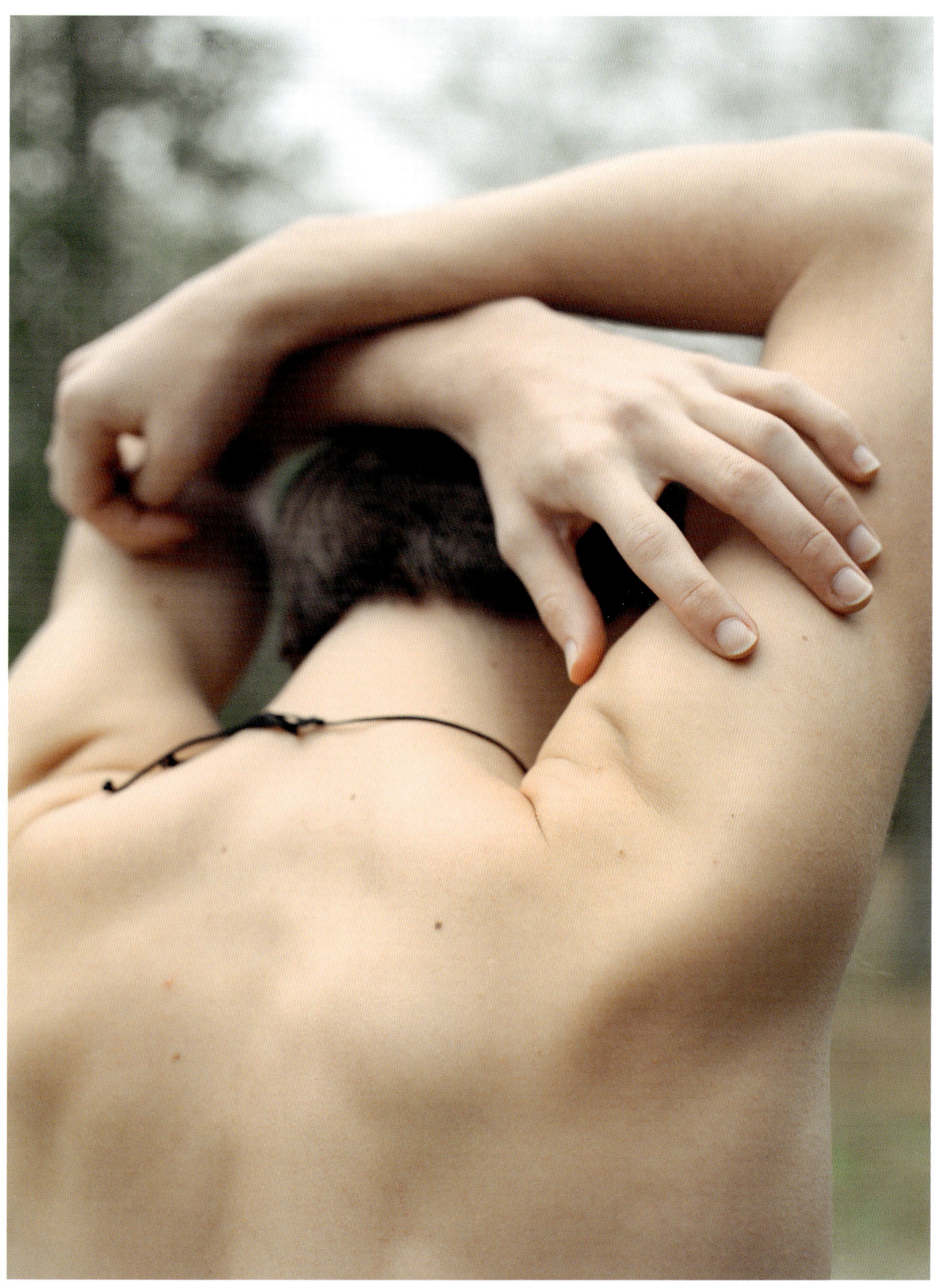

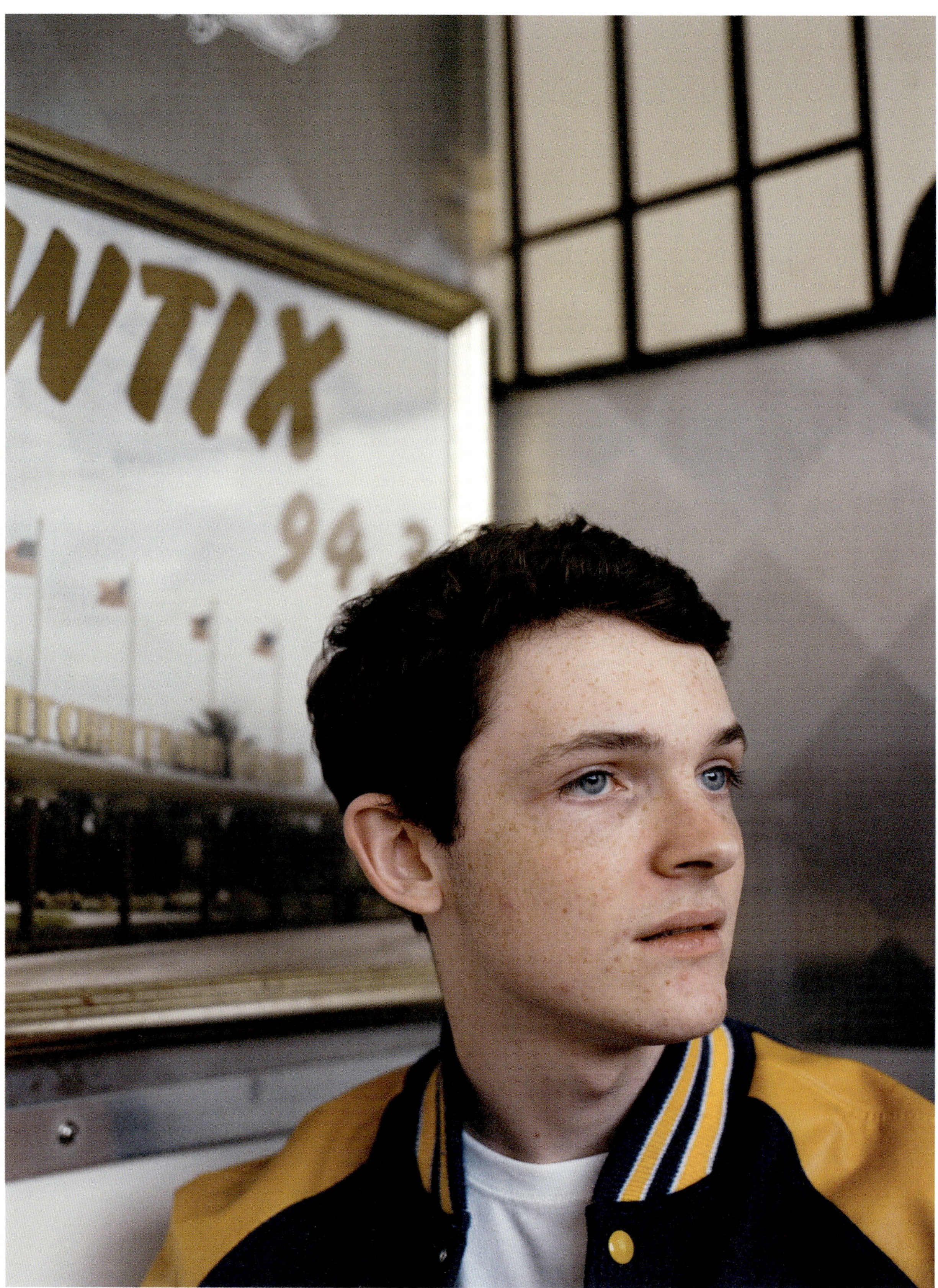
NTIX
94.2

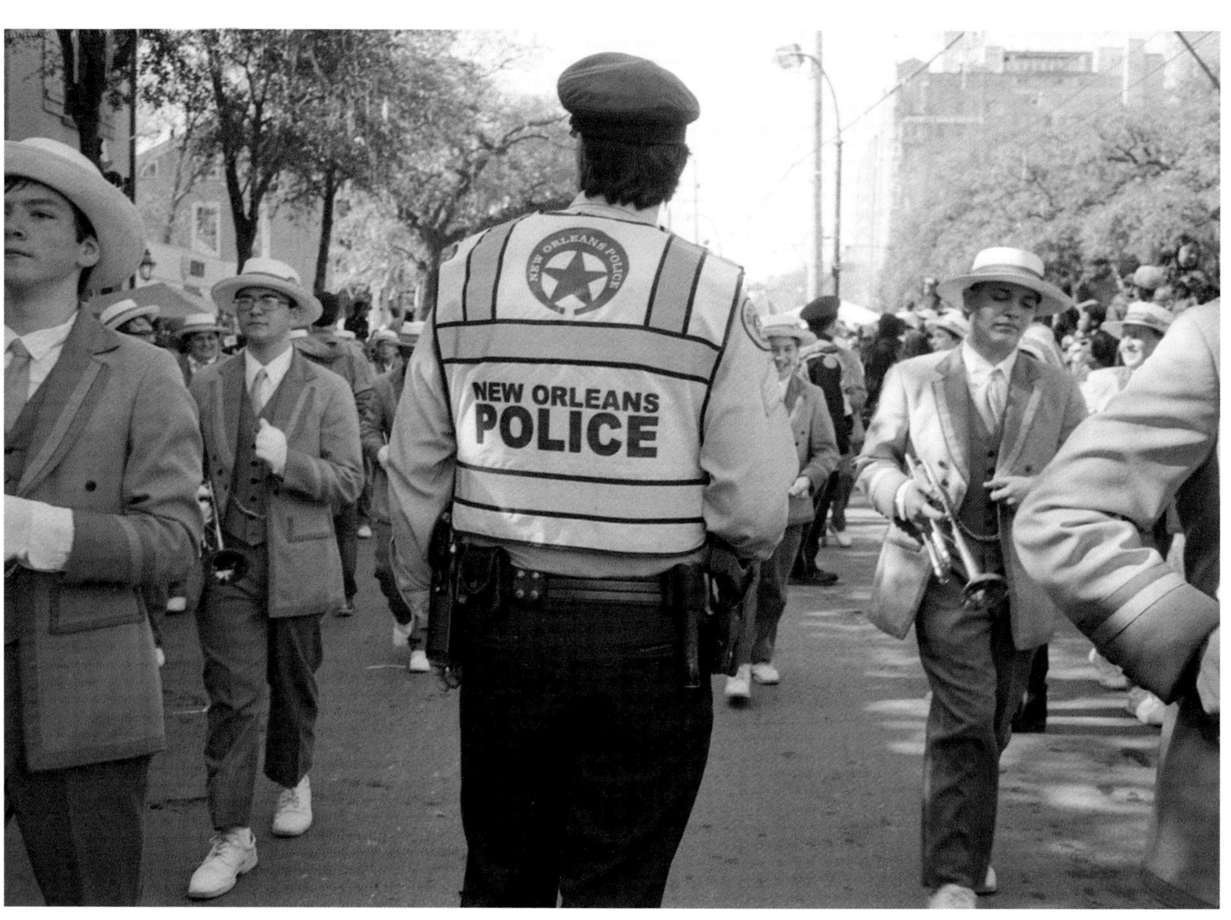
NEW ORLEANS POLICE
NEW ORLEANS
POLICE

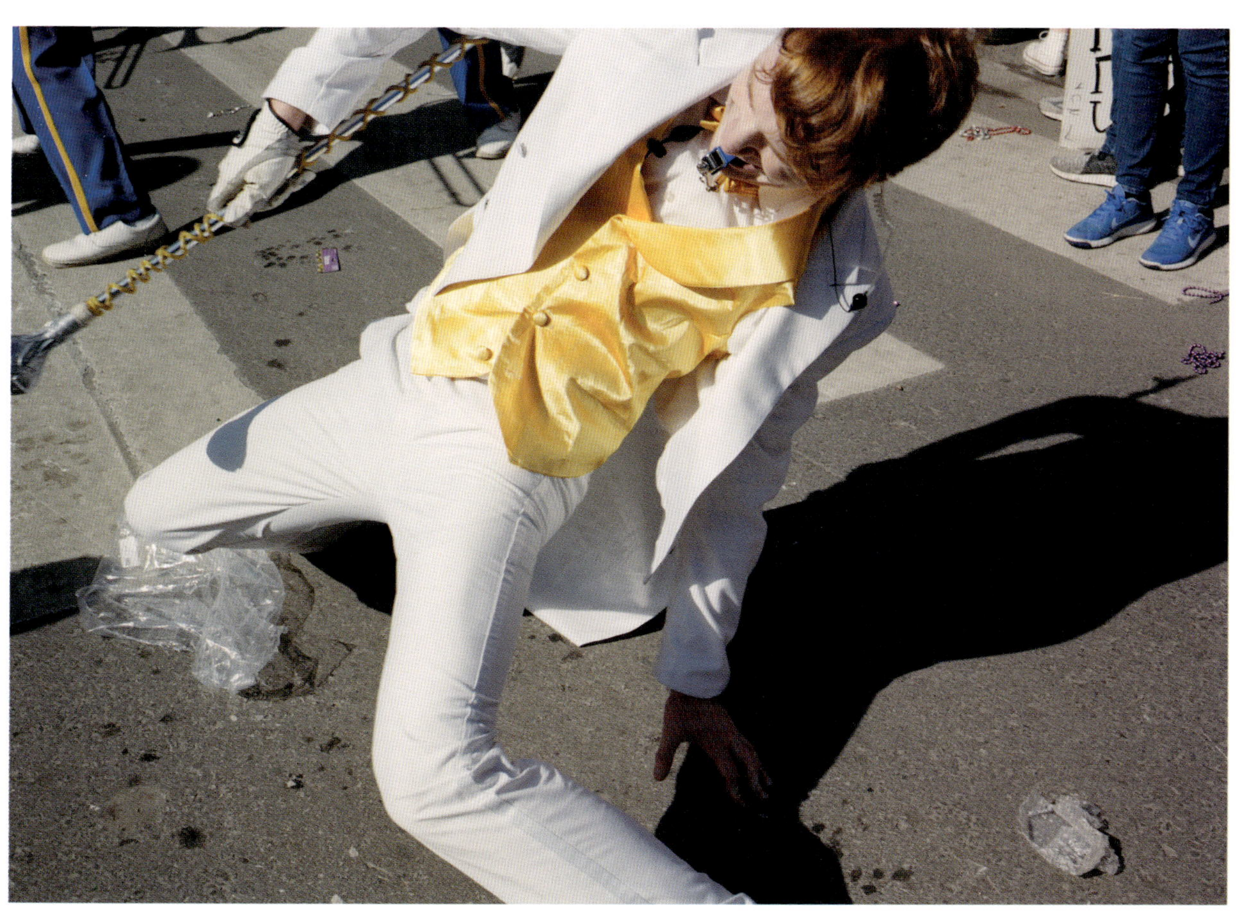

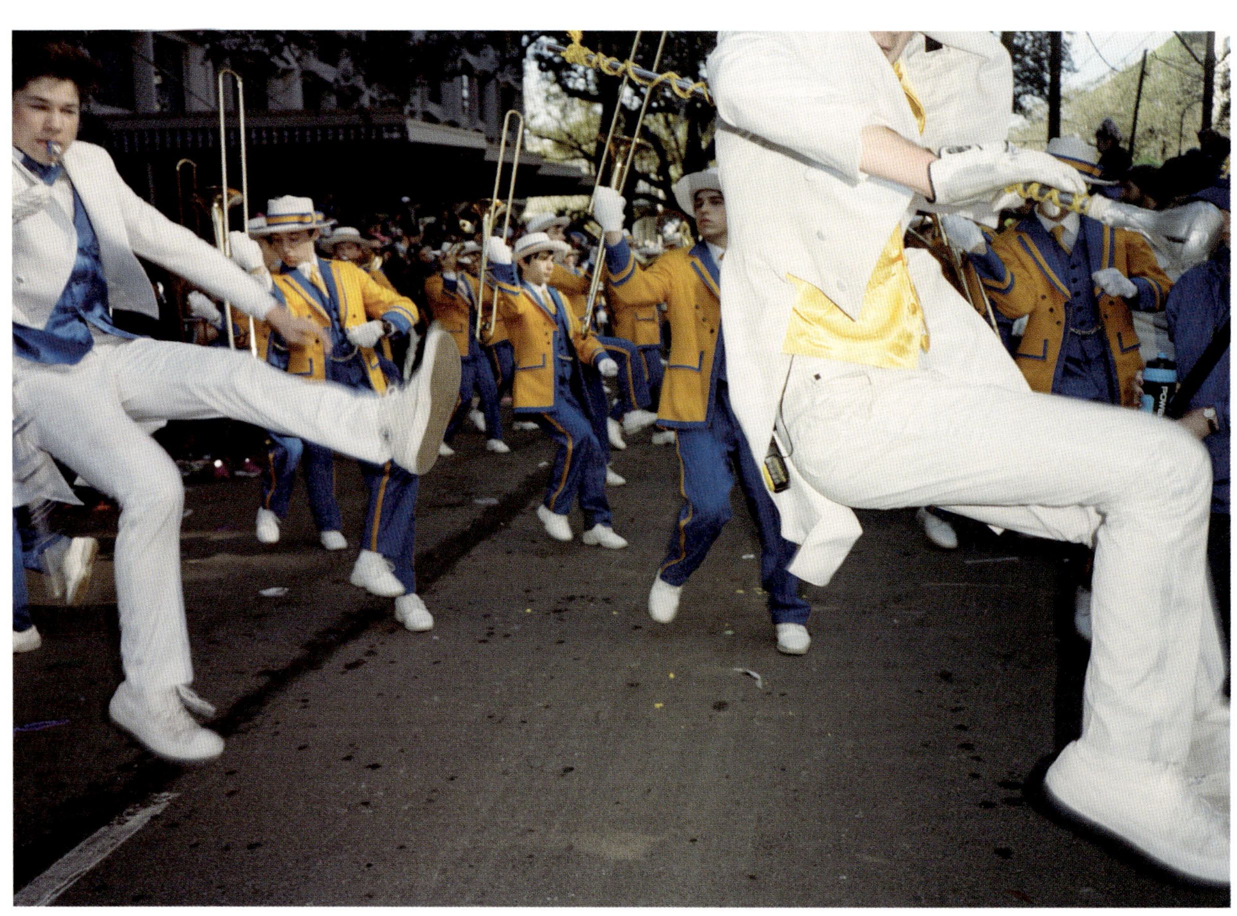

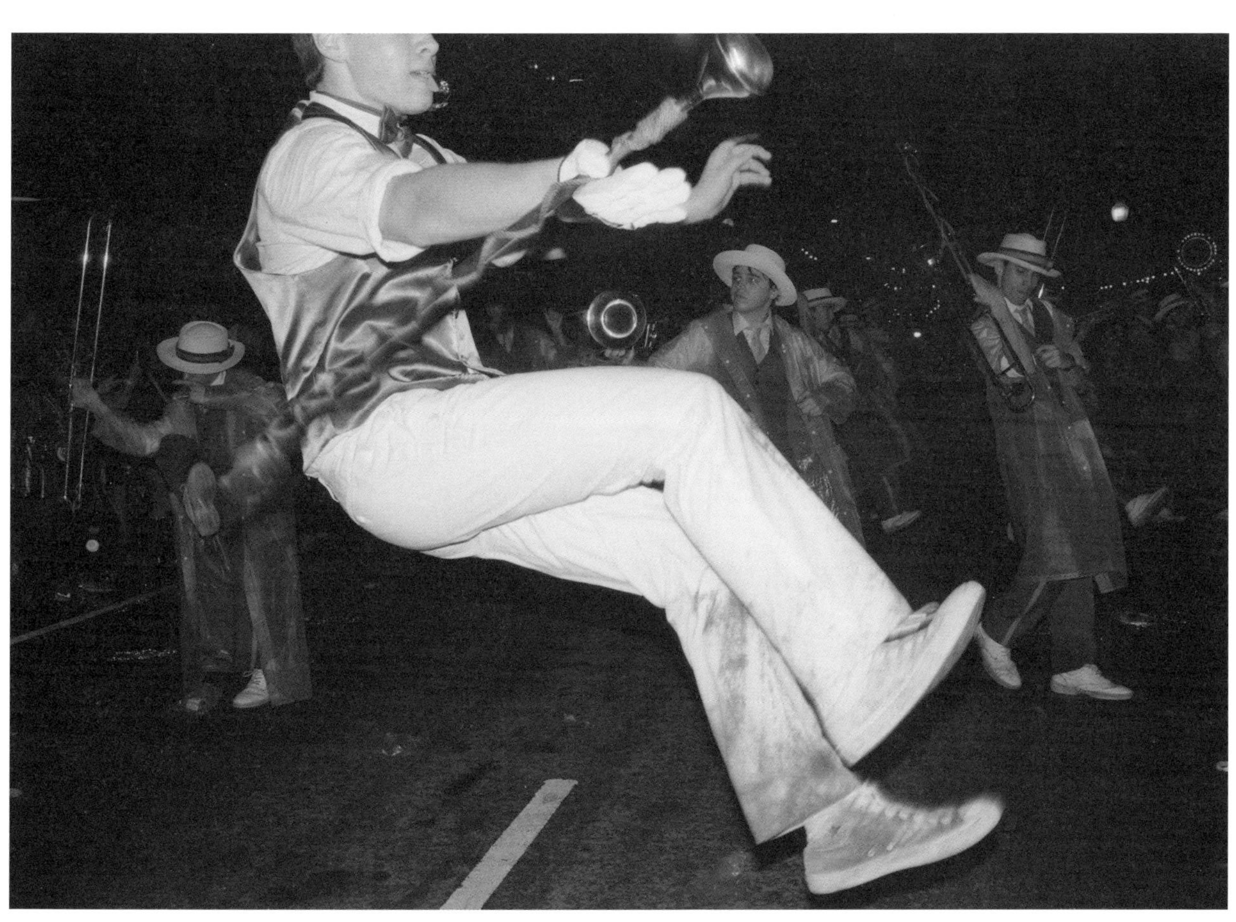

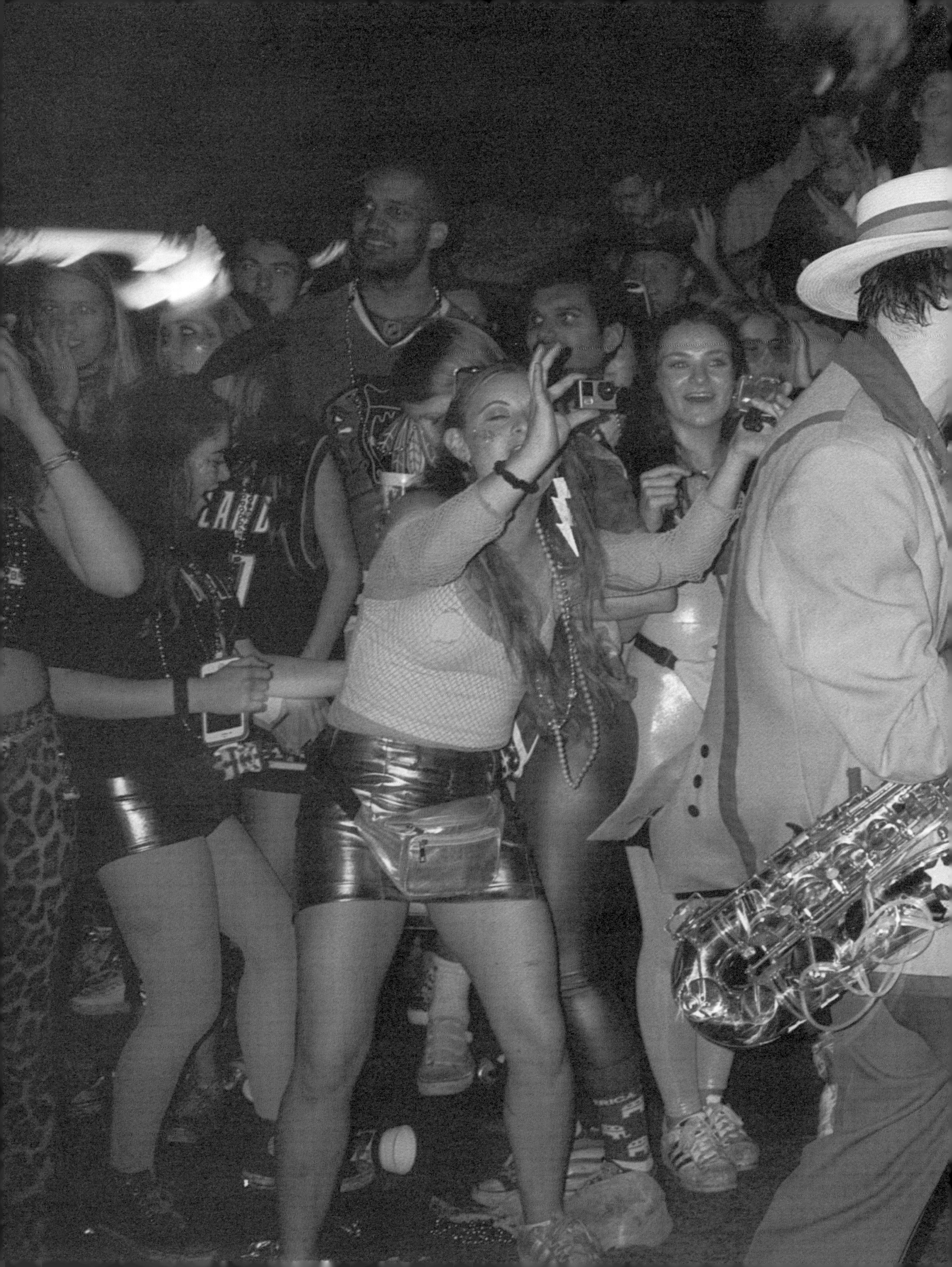

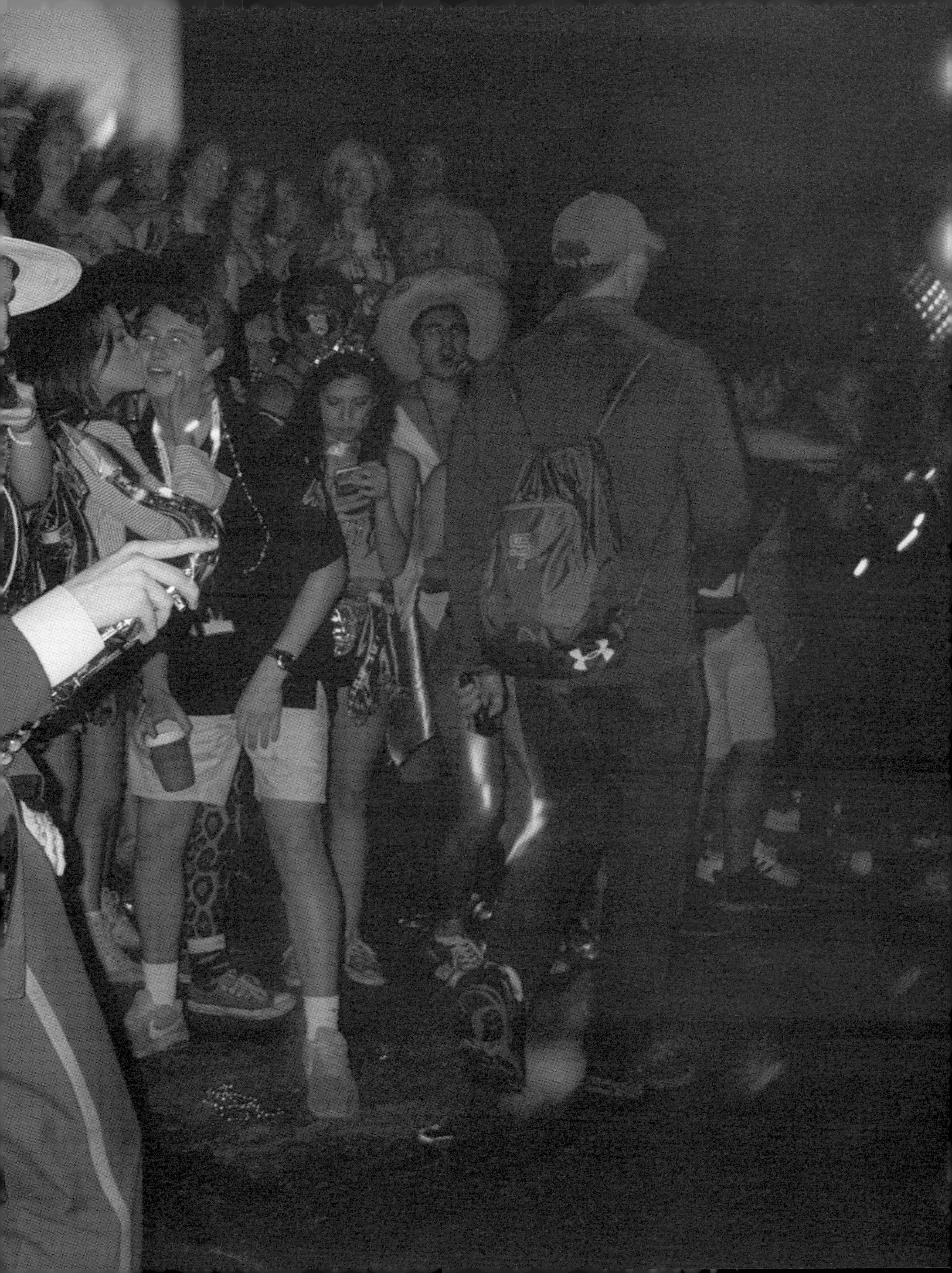

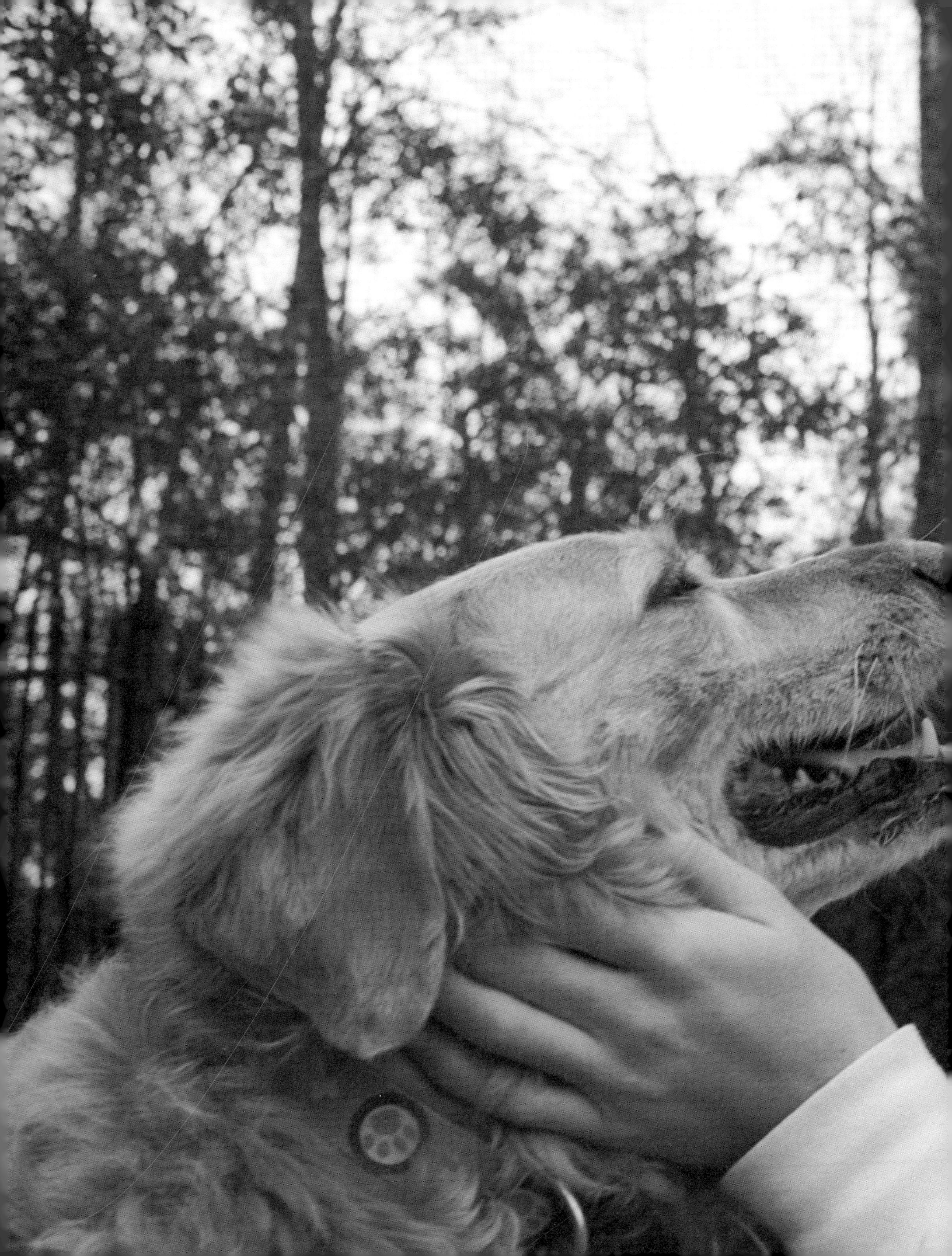

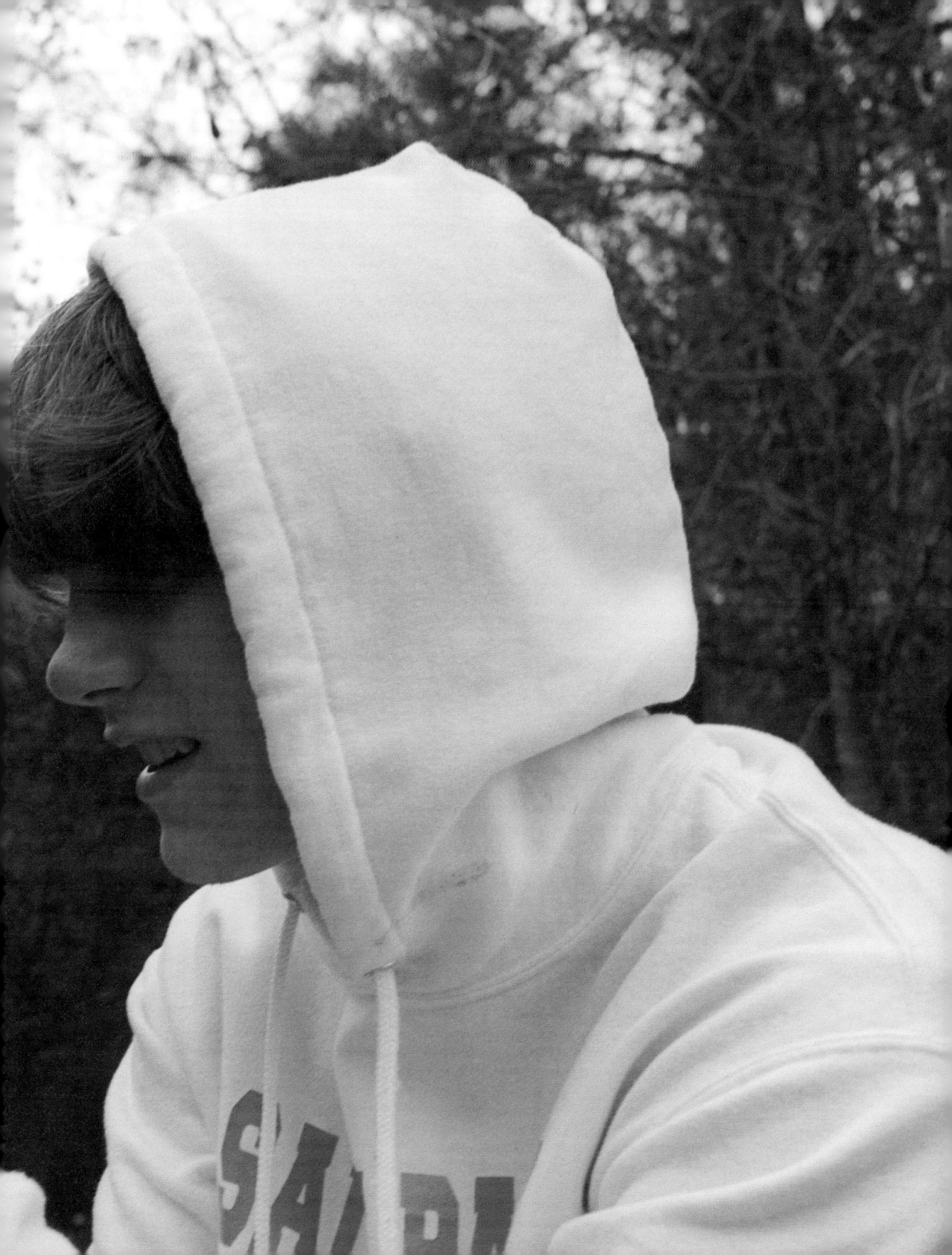
SAD B

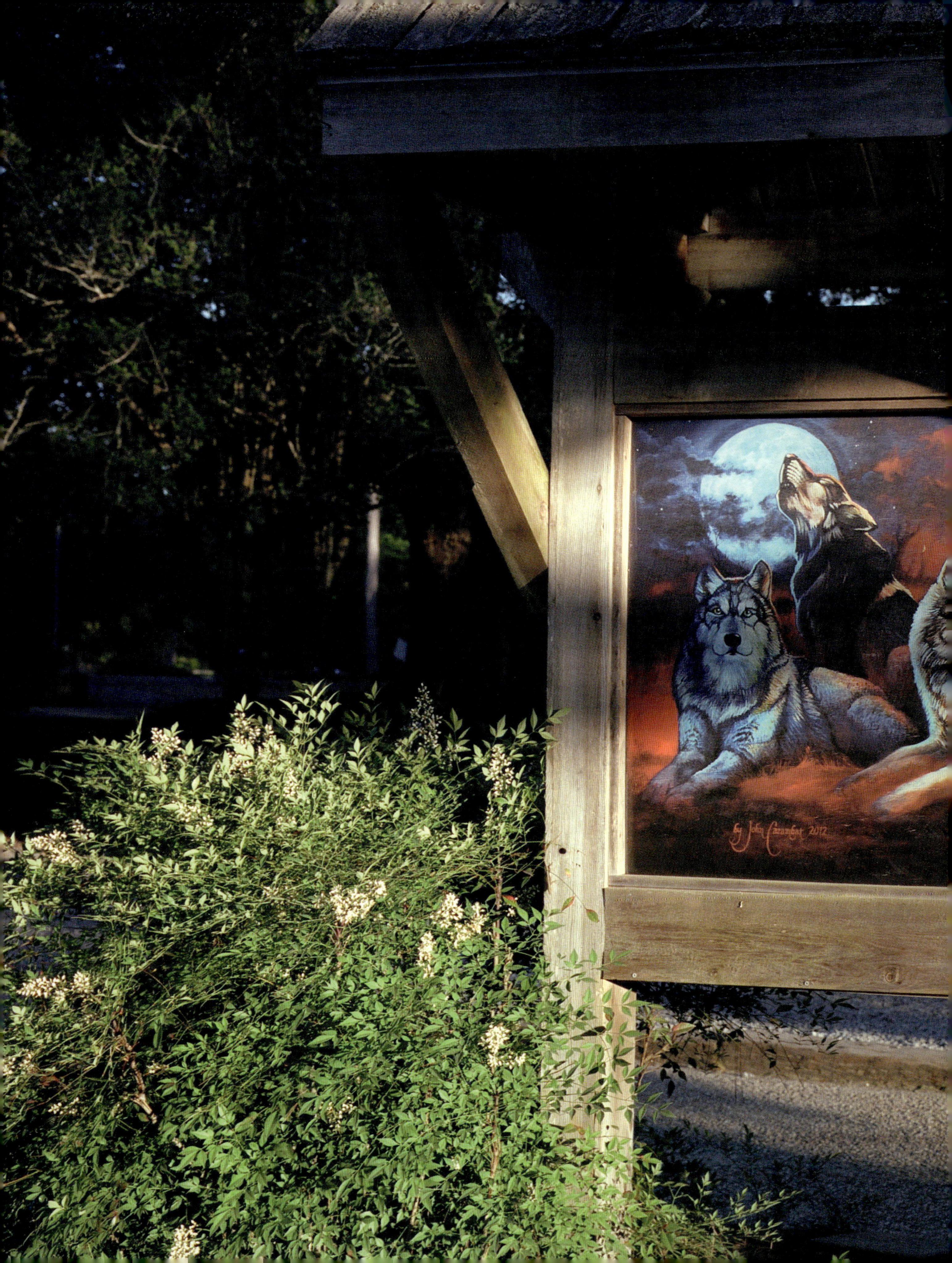

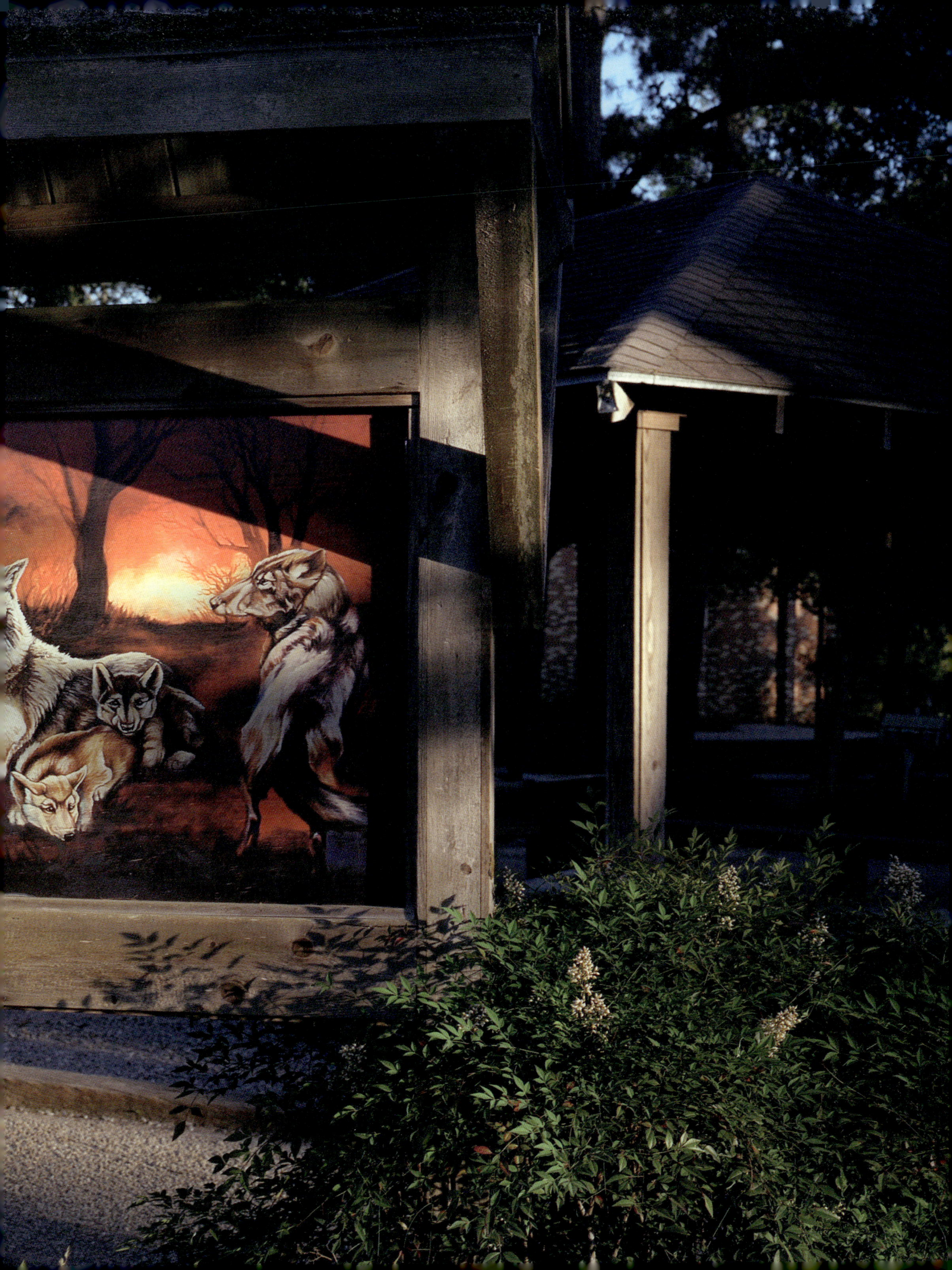

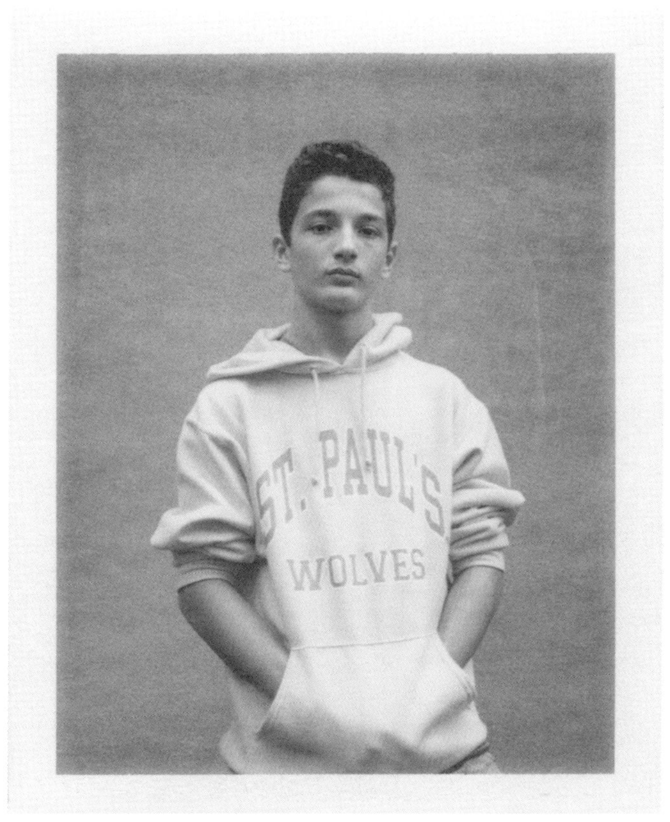

ST. PAUL'S
WOLVES

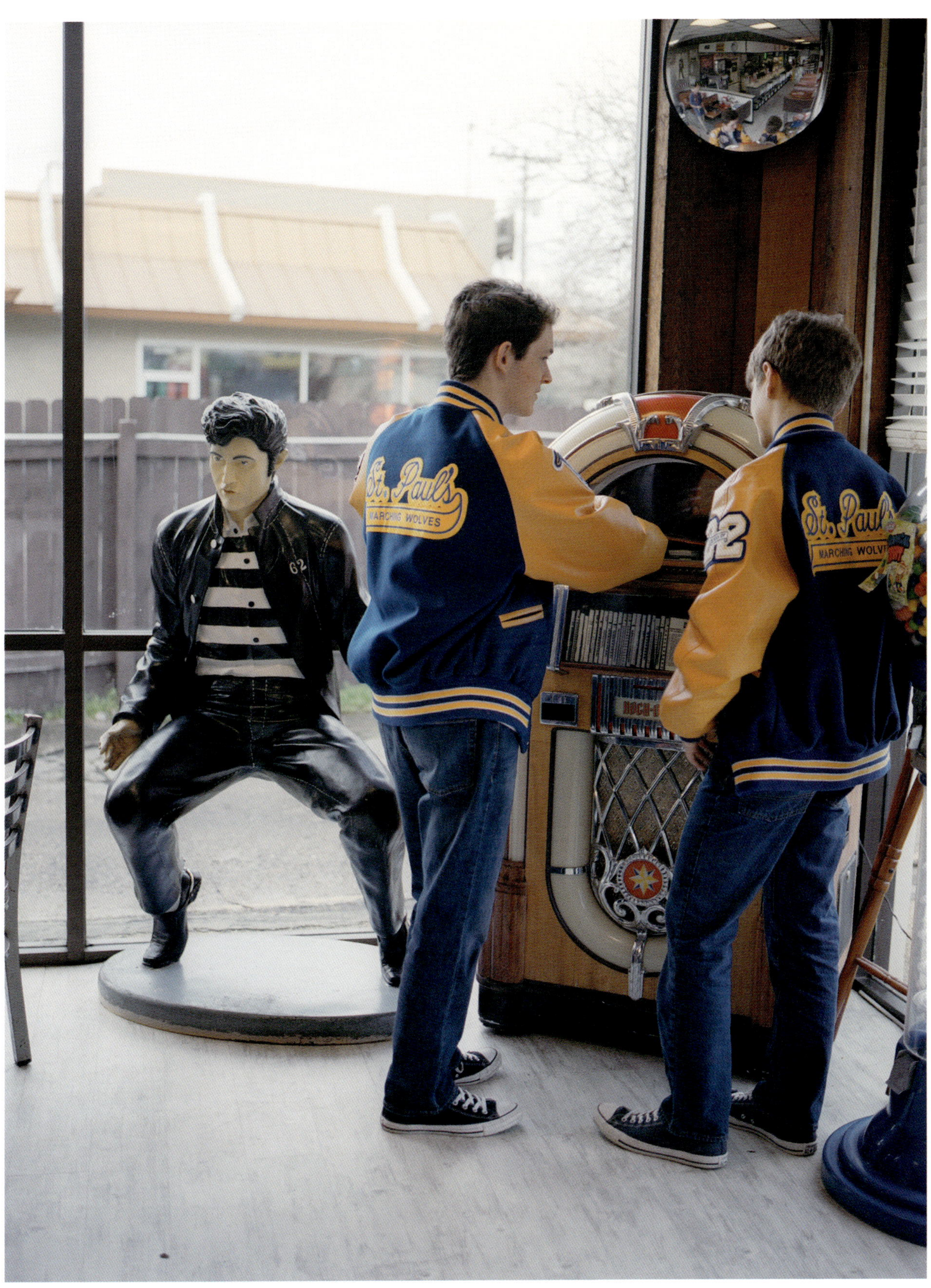

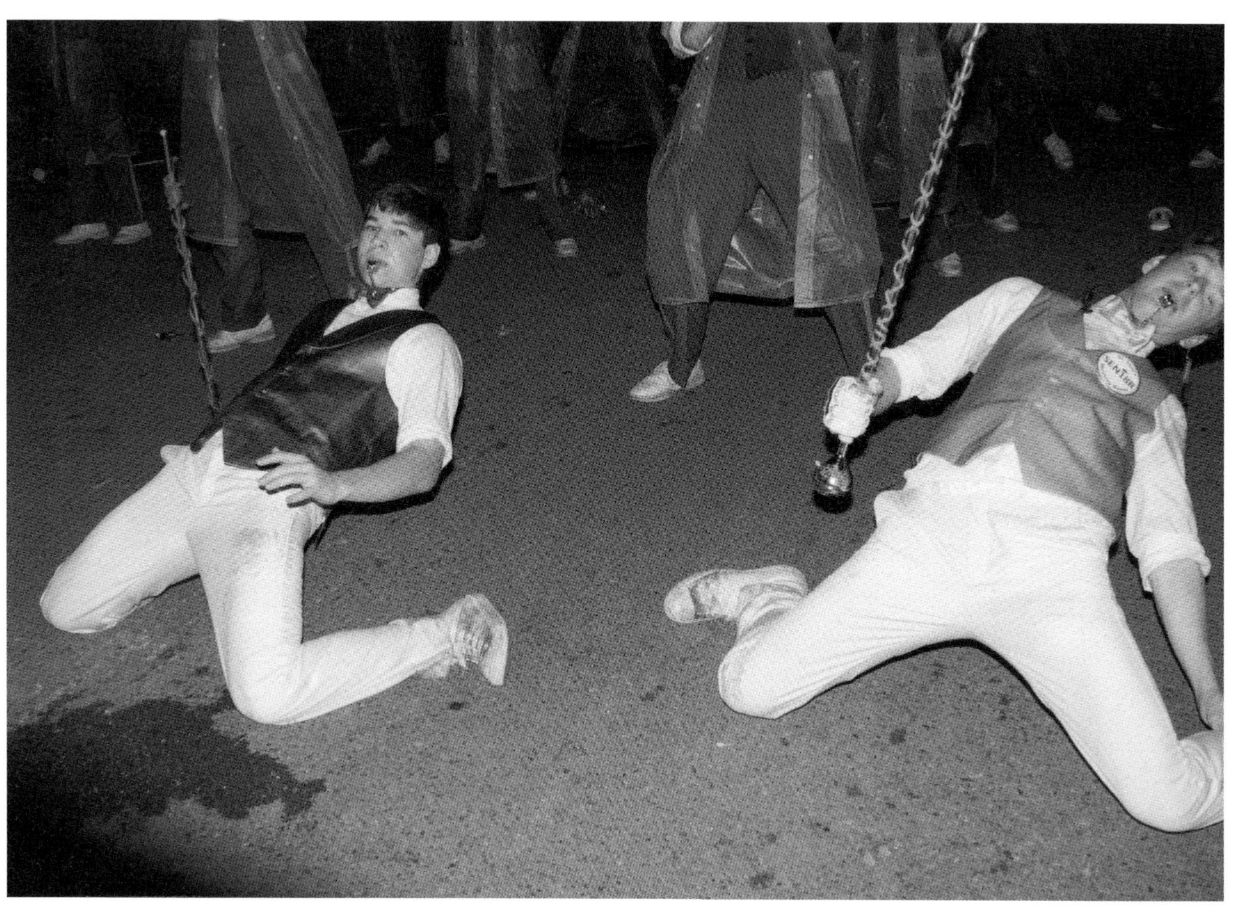

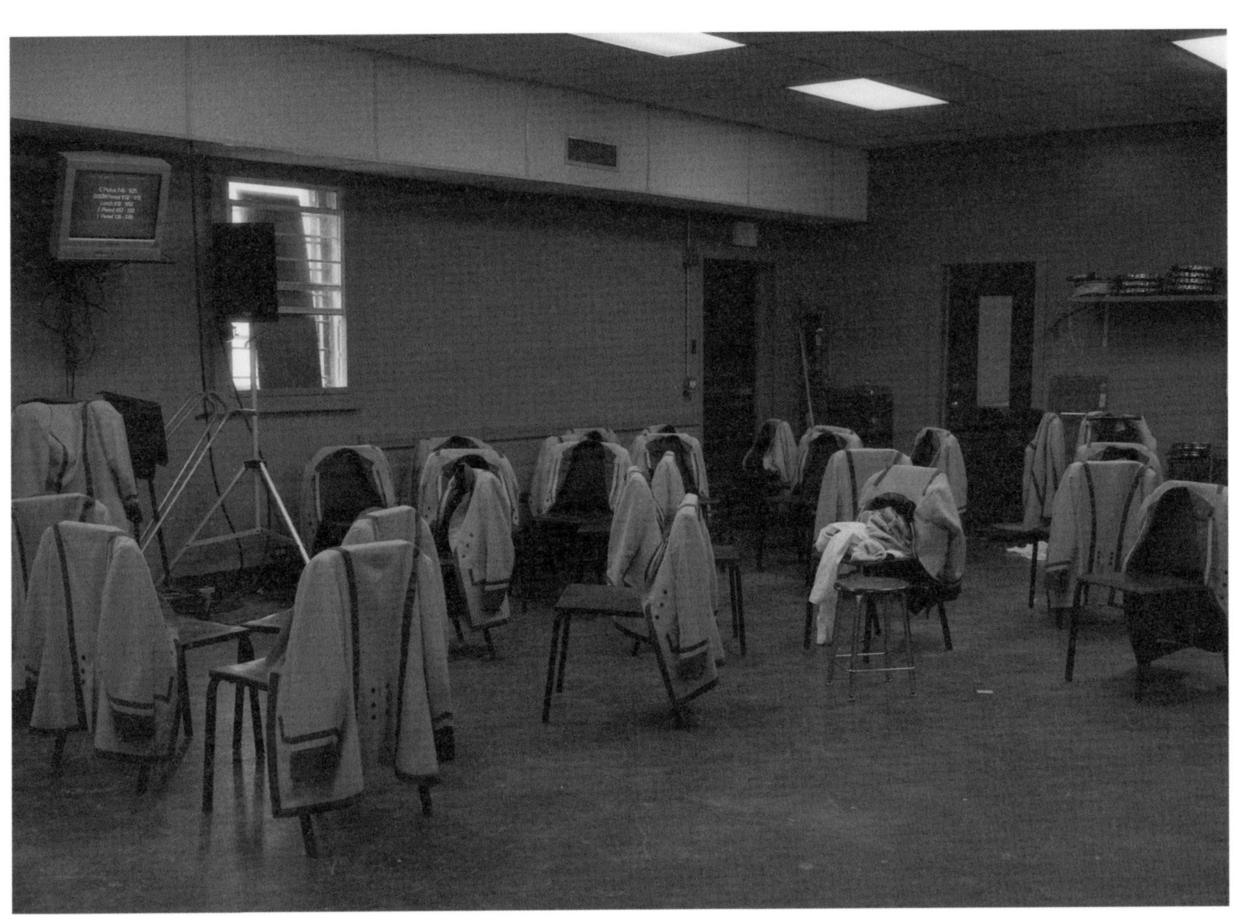

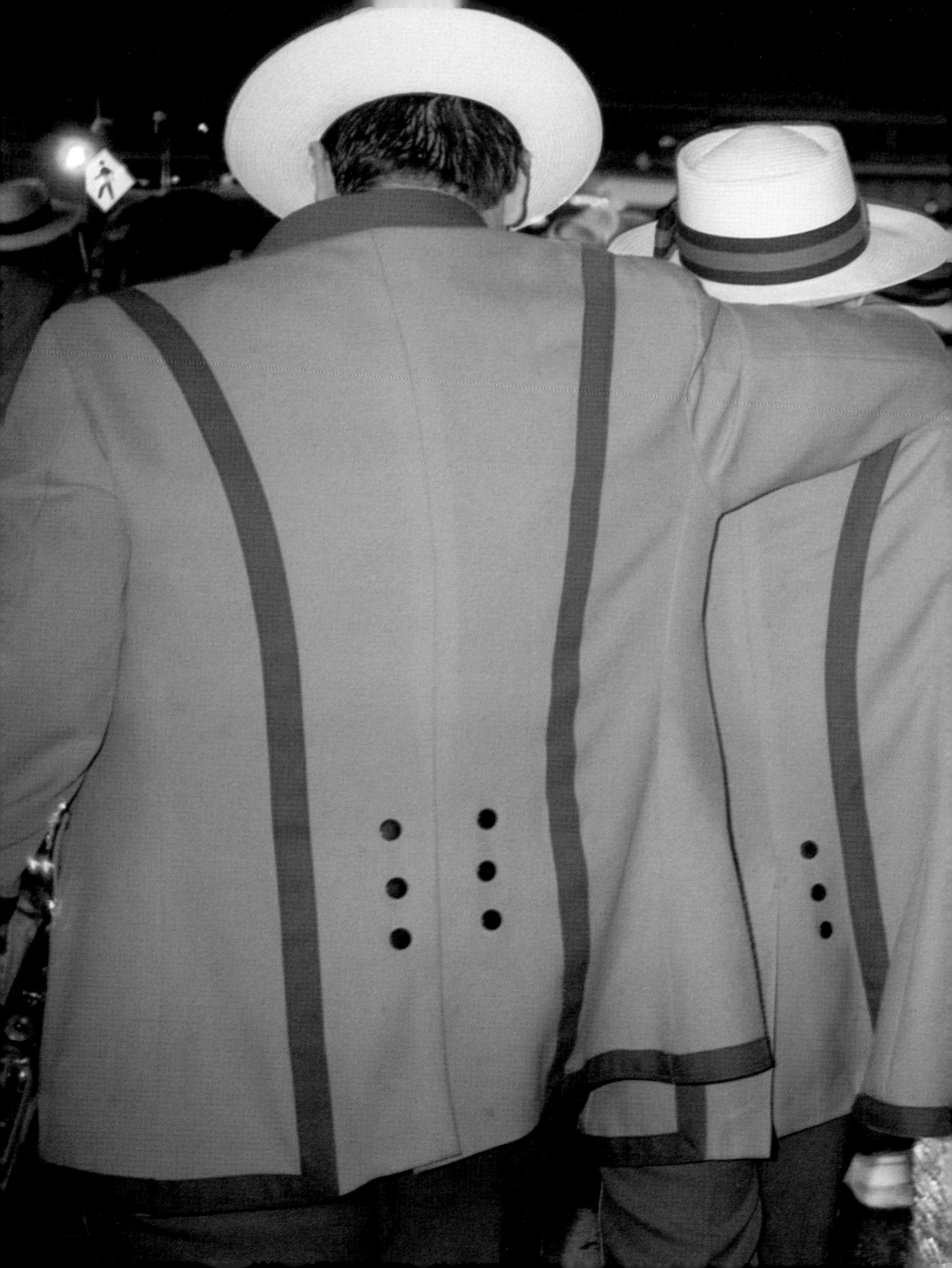

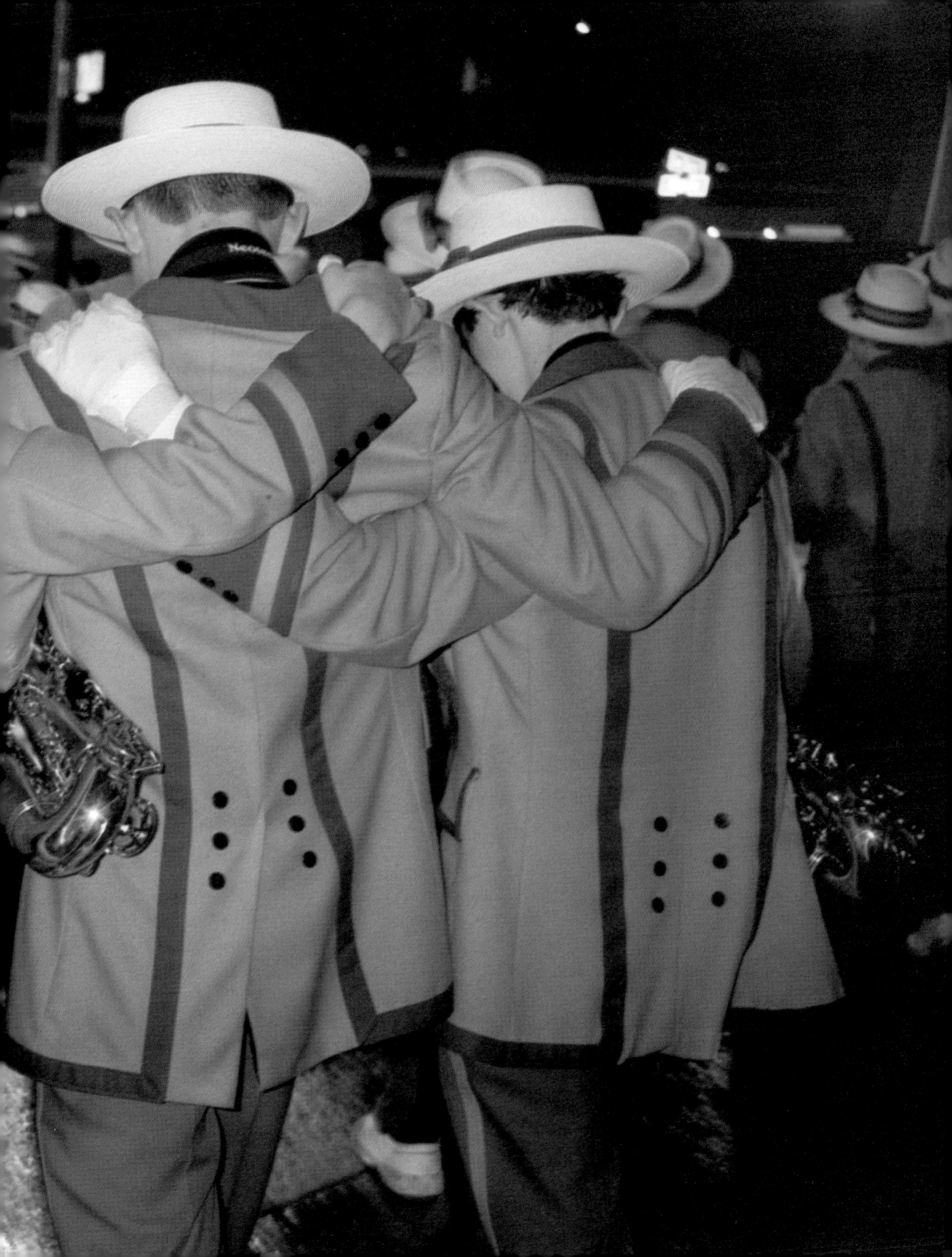

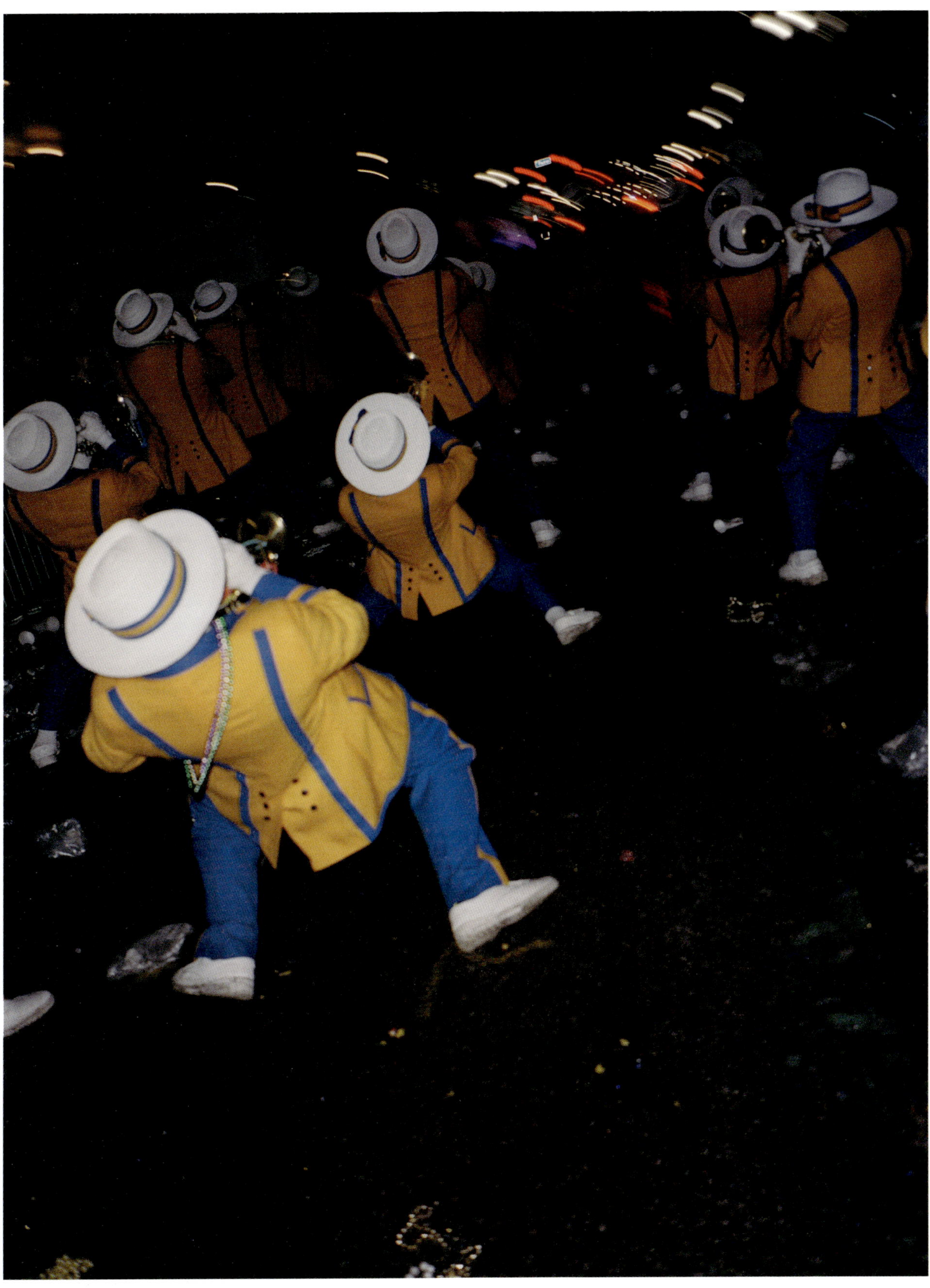

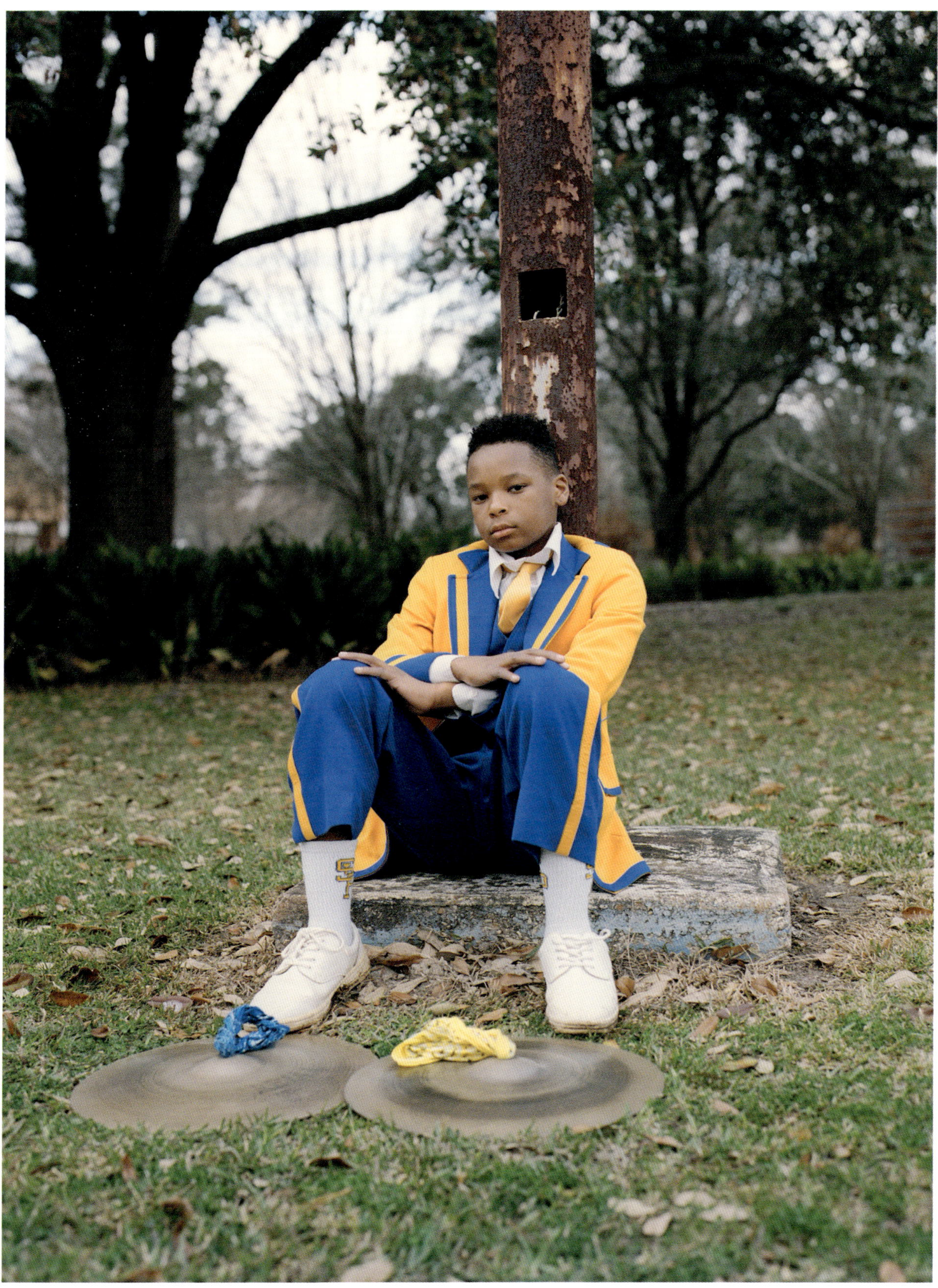

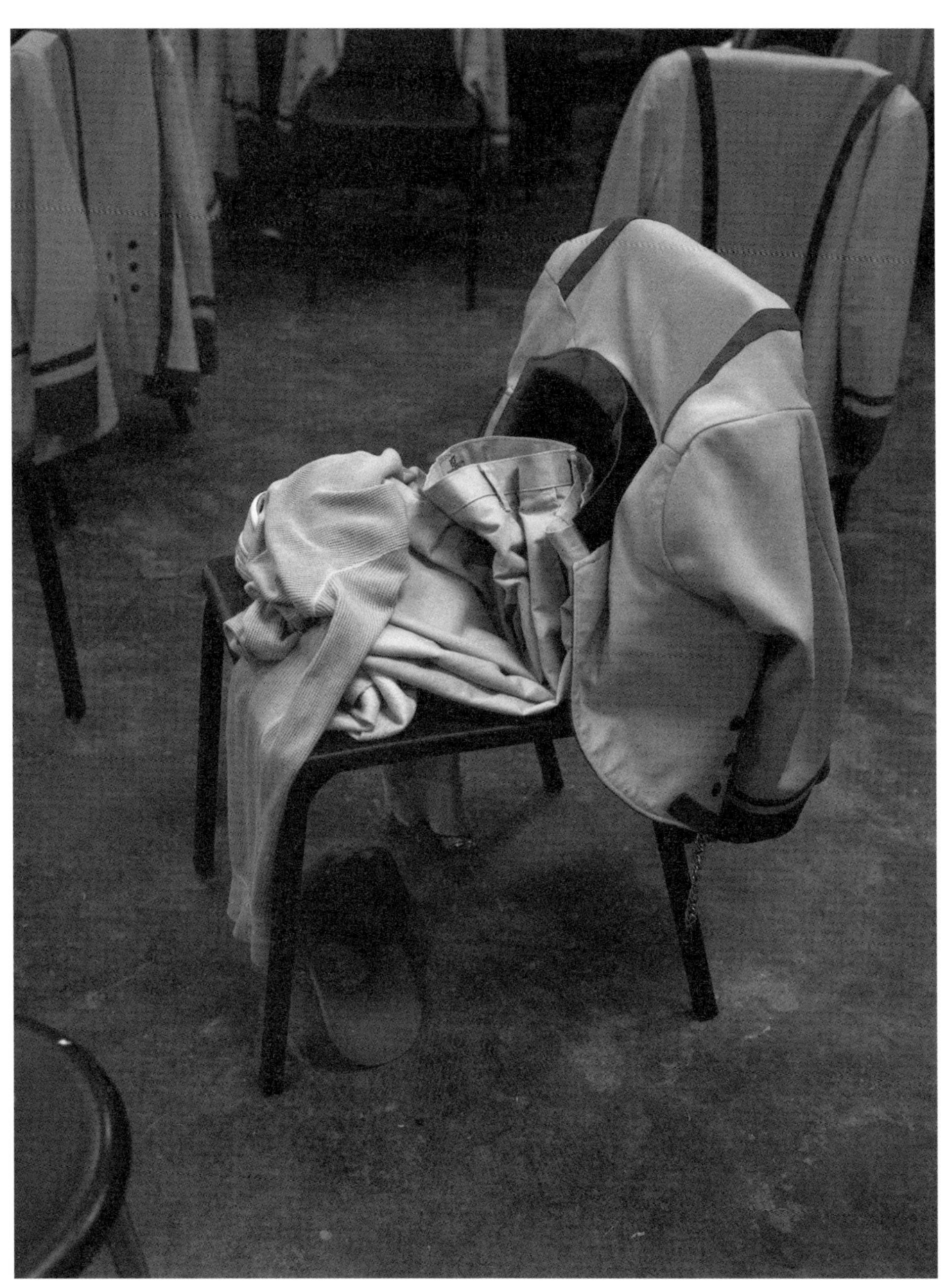

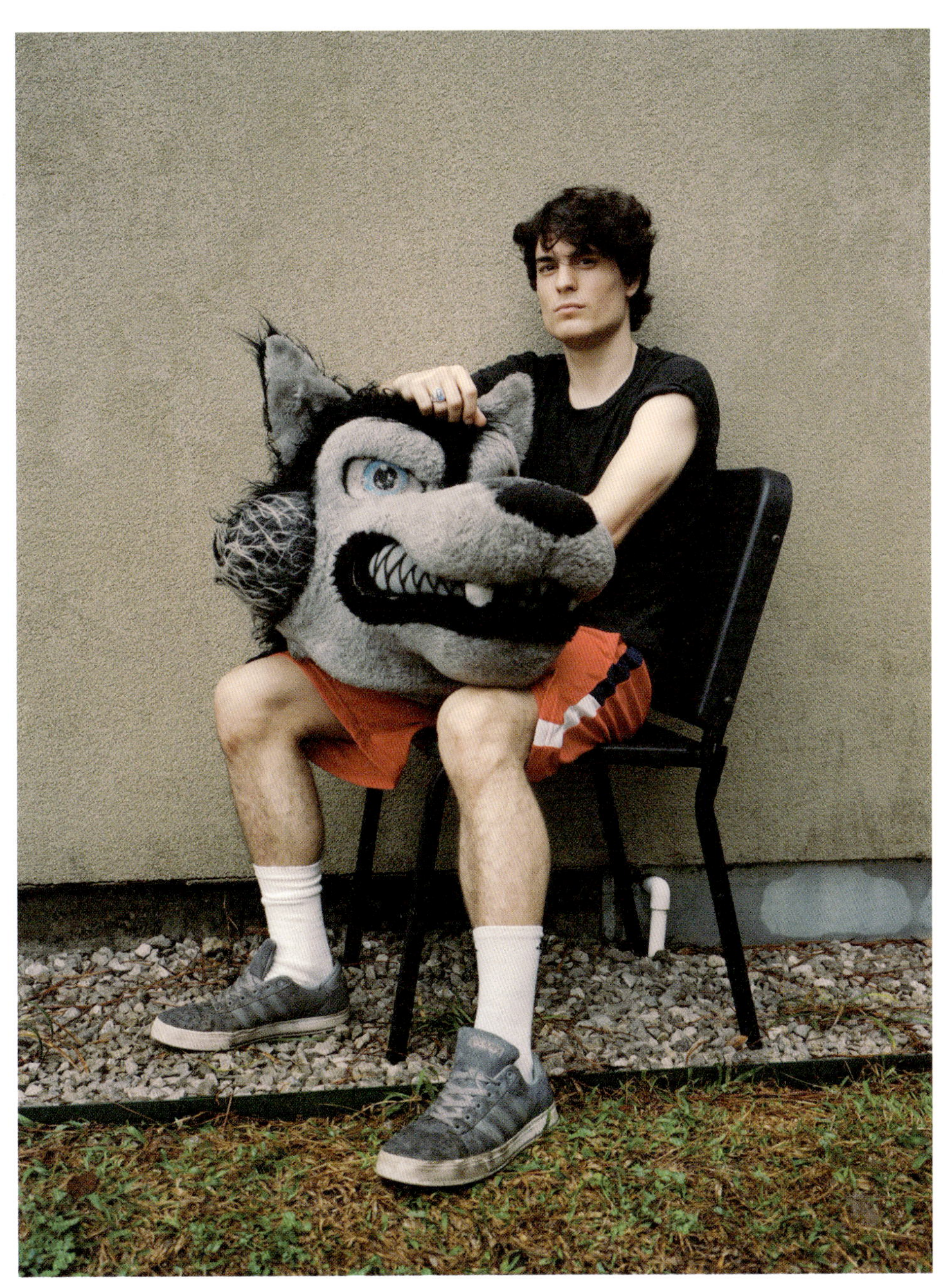

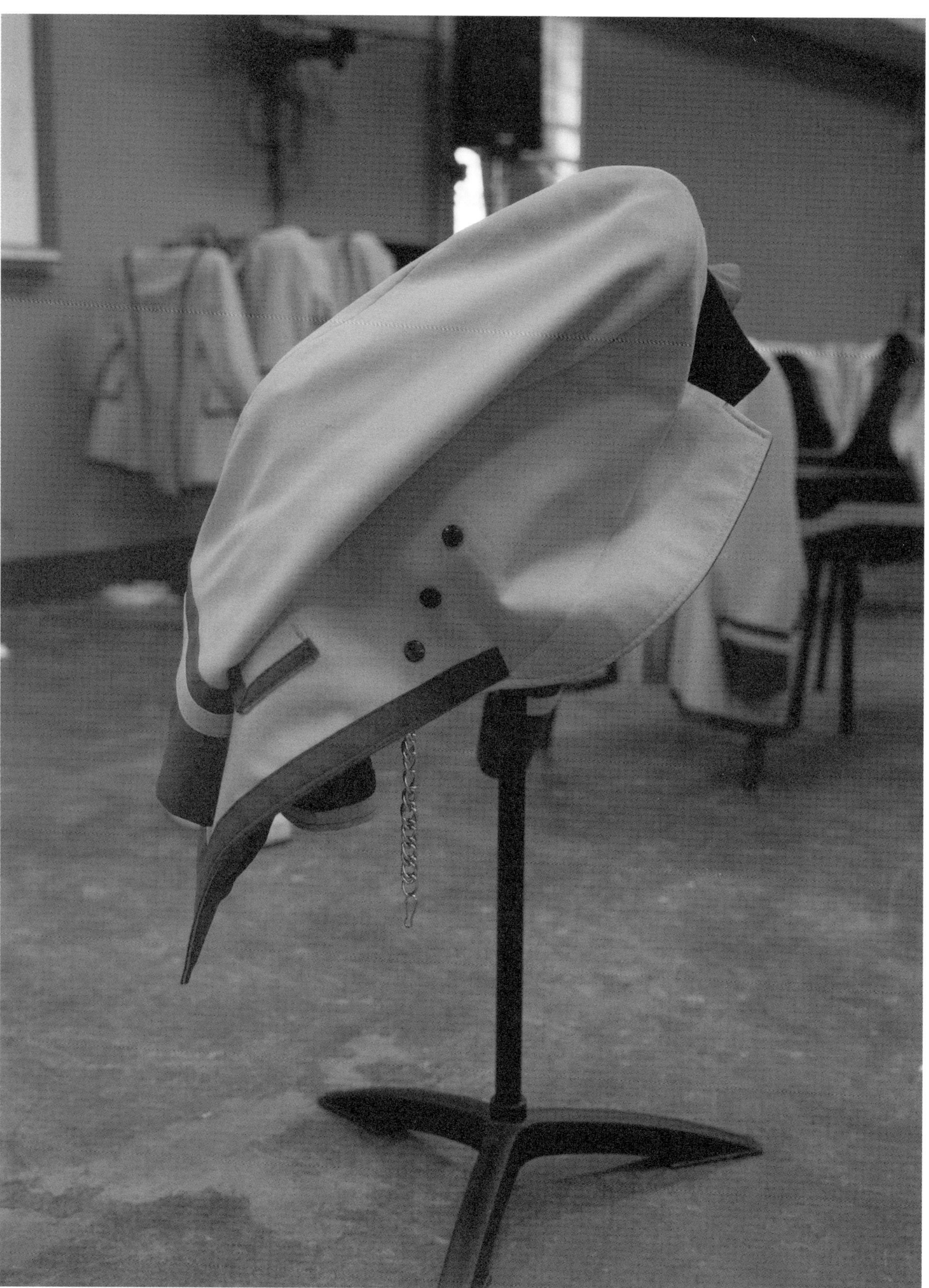

This book is dedicated to Matt Irwin (1980-2016)

Special thanks to everyone who made this project possible.
The Marching Wolves and their parents, Saint Paul's High School,
Andrew Moran, Ben Toms, Eduardo Silva, Christina Flannery, Susan and Greg Moran, Lian Calvo,
Sarah Kahloun, Jérémy Vitté and my family.

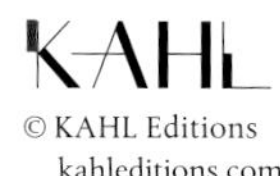

© KAHL Editions
kahleditions.com

© Photographs Fumi Nagasaka

Published by KAHL Editions ltd.
Editor   Sarah Kahloun
Art director   Jérémy Vitté
Design   KAHL Editions

Printed in October 2022 by KAHL Printing

First edition 2022
Edition of 500 copies,
including 50 numbered collector's editions.

ISBN 978-1-7398813-3-7

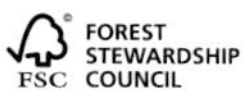